THE KEY
STUDENT STUDY GUIDE

THE KEY student study guide is designed to help students achieve success in school. The content in each study guide is 100% curriculum aligned and serves as an excellent source of material for review and practice. To create this book, teachers, curriculum specialists, and assessment experts have worked closely to develop the instructional pieces that explain each of the key concepts for the course. The practice questions and sample tests have detailed solutions that show problem-solving methods, highlight concepts that are likely to be tested, and point out potential sources of errors. **THE KEY** is a complete guide to be used by students throughout the school year for reviewing and understanding course content, and to prepare for assessments.

Rao, Gautam, 1961 –
THE KEY –Social Studies 30-1 Alberta

   1. Social Studies – Juvenile Literature. I. Title

ISBN: 978-1-77044-463-8
Published by
Castle Rock Research Corp.
2410 Manulife Place
10180 – 101 Street
Edmonton, AB T5J 3S4

10 9 8 7 6 5

Publisher
Gautam Rao

Contributors
Douglas Burns
Brigitta Goerres
Heather Friedenthal
Kelly Dury Laffin
James Kropfreiter
Richard Walker
Lois Westerlund

CASTLE ROCK
RESEARCH CORP

Dedicated to the memory of Dr. V. S. Rao

THE KEY—Social Studies 30-1

THE KEY consists of the following sections:

KEY Tips for Being Successful at School gives examples of study and review strategies. It includes information about learning styles, study schedules, and note taking for test preparation.

Class Focus includes a unit on each area of the curriculum. Units are divided into sections, each focusing on one of the specific expectations, or main ideas, that students must learn about in that unit. Examples, definitions, and visuals help to explain each main idea. Practice questions on the main ideas are also included. At the end of each unit is a test on the important ideas covered. The practice questions and unit tests help students identify areas they know and those they need to study more. They can also be used as preparation for tests and quizzes. Most questions are of average difficulty, though some are easy and some are hard. Each unit is prefaced by a *Table of Correlations*, which correlates questions in the unit (and in the practice tests at the end of the book) to the specific curriculum expectations. Answers and solutions are found at the end of each unit.

KEY Strategies for Success on Tests helps students get ready for tests. It shows students different types of questions they might see, word clues to look for when reading them, and hints for answering them.

Practice Tests includes one to three tests based on the entire course. They are very similar to the format and level of difficulty that students may encounter on final tests. In some regions, these tests may be reprinted versions of official tests, or reflect the same difficulty levels and formats as official versions. This gives students the chance to practice using real-world examples. Answers and complete solutions are provided at the end of the section.

For the complete curriculum document (including specific expectations along with examples and sample problems), visit http://education.alberta.ca/teachers/program/socialstudies/programs.aspx

THE KEY Study Guides are available for many courses. Check www.castlerockresearch.com for a complete listing of books available for your area.

For information about any of our resources or services, please call Castle Rock Research at 780.448.9619 or visit our website at http://www.castlerockresearch.com.

At Castle Rock Research, we strive to produce an error-free resource. If you should find an error, please contact us so that future editions can be corrected.

TABLE OF CONTENTS

KEY Tips for being Successful at School

KEY TIPS FOR BEING SUCCESSFUL AT SCHOOL

KEY FACTORS CONTRIBUTING TO SCHOOL SUCCESS

In addition to learning the content of your courses, there are some other things that you can do to help you do your best at school. You can try some of the following strategies:

- **Keep a positive attitude**: Always reflect on what you can already do and what you already know.

- **Be prepared to learn**: Have the necessary pencils, pens, notebooks, and other required materials for participating in class ready.

- **Complete all of your assignments**: Do your best to finish all of your assignments. Even if you know the material well, practice will reinforce your knowledge. If an assignment or question is difficult for you, work through it as far as you can so that your teacher can see exactly where you are having difficulty.

- **Set small goals for yourself when you are learning new material**: For example, when learning the parts of speech, do not try to learn everything in one night. Work on only one part or section each study session. When you have memorized one particular part of speech and understand it, move on to another one. Continue this process until you have memorized and learned all the parts of speech.

- **Review your classroom work regularly at home**: Review to make sure you understand the material you learned in class.

- **Ask your teacher for help**: Your teacher will help you if you do not understand something or if you are having a difficult time completing your assignments.

- **Get plenty of rest and exercise**: Concentrating in class is hard work. It is important to be well-rested and have time to relax and socialize with your friends. This helps you keep a positive attitude about your schoolwork.

- **Eat healthy meals**: A balanced diet keeps you healthy and gives you the energy you need for studying at school and at home.

HOW TO FIND YOUR LEARNING STYLE

Every student learns differently. The manner in which you learn best is called your learning style. By knowing your learning style, you can increase your success at school. Most students use a combination of learning styles. Do you know what type of learner you are? Read the following descriptions. Which of these common learning styles do you use most often?

- Linguistic Learner: You may learn best by saying, hearing, and seeing words. You are probably really good at memorizing things such as dates, places, names, and facts. You may need to write down the steps in a process, a formula, or the actions that lead up to a significant event, and then say them out loud.

- Spatial Learner: You may learn best by looking at and working with pictures. You are probably really good at puzzles, imagining things, and reading maps and charts. You may need to use strategies like mind mapping and webbing to organize your information and study notes.

- Kinesthetic Learner: You may learn best by touching, moving, and figuring things out using manipulatives. You are probably really good at physical activities and learning through movement. You may need to draw your finger over a diagram to remember it, tap out the steps needed to solve a problem, or feel yourself writing or typing a formula.

SCHEDULING STUDY TIME

You should review your class notes regularly to ensure that you have a clear understanding of all the new material you learned. Reviewing your lessons on a regular basis helps you to learn and remember ideas and concepts. It also reduces the quantity of material that you need to study prior to a test. Establishing a study schedule will help you to make the best use of your time.

• Regardless of the type of study schedule you use, you may want to consider the following suggestions to maximize your study time and effort:

• Organize your work so that you begin with the most challenging material first.

• Divide the subject's content into small, manageable chunks.

• Alternate regularly between your different subjects and types of study activities in order to maintain your interest and motivation.

• Make a daily list with headings like "Must Do," "Should Do," and "Could Do."

• Begin each study session by quickly reviewing what you studied the day before.

• Maintain your usual routine of eating, sleeping, and exercising to help you concentrate better for extended periods of time.

CREATING STUDY NOTES

MIND-MAPPING OR WEBBING

Use the key words, ideas, or concepts from your class notes to create a mind map or web, which is a diagram or visual representation of the given information. A mind map or web is sometimes referred to as a knowledge map. Use the following steps to create a mind map or web:

1. Write the key word, concept, theory, or formula in the centre of your page.

2. Write down related facts, ideas, events, and information, and link them to the central concept with lines.

3. Use coloured markers, underlining, or symbols to emphasize things such as relationships, timelines, and important information.

The following mind map is an example of one that could help you develop an essay:

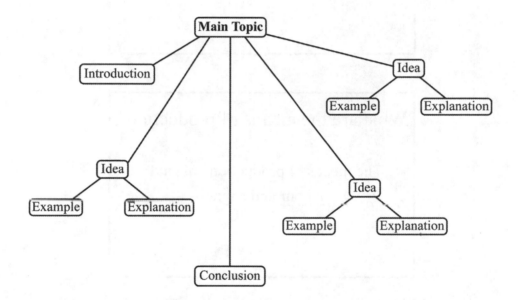

INDEX CARDS

To use index cards while studying, follow these steps:

1. Write a key word or question on one side of an index card.

2. On the reverse side, write the definition of the word, answer to the question, or any other important information that you want to remember.

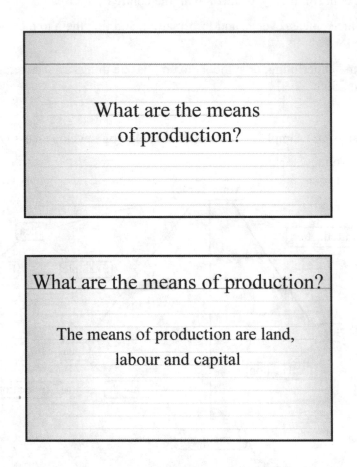

SYMBOLS AND STICKY NOTES—IDENTIFYING IMPORTANT INFORMATION

Use symbols to mark your class notes. For example, an exclamation mark (!) might be used to point out something that must be learned well because it is a very important idea. A question mark (?) may highlight something you are not certain about, and a diamond (◊) or asterisk (*) could highlight interesting information that you want to remember. Sticky notes are useful in the following situations:

- Use sticky notes when you are not allowed to put marks in books.

- Use sticky notes to mark a page in a book that contains an important diagram, formula, explanation, or other information.

- Use sticky notes to mark important facts in research books.

MEMORIZATION TECHNIQUES

The following techniques can help you when you need to memorize something:

- **Association** relates new learning to something you already know. For example, to remember the spelling difference between dessert and desert, recall that the word *sand* has only one *s*. So, because there is sand in a desert, the word *desert* has only one *s*.

- **Mnemonic** devices are sentences that you create to remember a list or group of items. For example, the first letter of each word in the phrase "**E**very **G**ood **B**oy **D**eserves **F**udge" helps you to remember the names of the lines on the treble-clef staff (E, G, B, D, and F) in music.

- **Acronyms** are words that are formed from the first letters or parts of the words in a group. For example, RADAR is actually an acronym for Radio Detecting and Ranging, and MASH is an acronym for Mobile Army Surgical Hospital. HOMES helps you to remember the names of the five Great Lakes (Huron, Ontario, Michigan, Erie, and Superior).

- **Visualizing** requires you to use your mind's eye to "see" a chart, list, map, diagram, or sentence as it is in your textbook or notes, on the chalkboard or computer screen, or in a display.

- **Initialisms** are abbreviations that are formed from the first letters or parts of the words in a group. Unlike acronyms, an initialism cannot be pronounced as a word itself. For example, BEDMAS is an initialism for the order of operations in math (Brackets, Exponents, Divide, Multiply, Add, Subtract).

KEY STRATEGIES FOR REVIEWING

Reviewing textbook material, class notes, and handouts should be an ongoing activity. Spending time reviewing becomes more critical when you are preparing for a test. You may find some of the following review strategies useful when studying during your scheduled study time:

- Before reading a selection, preview it by noting the headings, charts, graphs, and chapter questions.

- Before reviewing a unit, note the headings, charts, graphs, and chapter questions.

- Highlight key concepts, vocabulary, definitions, and formulas.

- Skim the paragraph, and note the key words, phrases, and information.

- Carefully read over each step in a procedure.

- Draw a picture or diagram to help make the concept clearer.

KEY STRATEGIES FOR SUCCESS: A CHECKLIST

Reviewing is a huge part of doing well at school and preparing for tests. Here is a checklist for you to keep track of how many suggested strategies for success you are using. Read each question, and put a check mark (✓) in the correct column. Look at the questions where you have checked the "No" column. Think about how you might try using some of these strategies to help you do your best at school.

KEY Strategies for Success	Yes	No
Do you attend school regularly?		
Do you know your personal learning style—how you learn best?		
Do you spend 15 to 30 minutes a day reviewing your notes?		
Do you study in a quiet place at home?		
Do you clearly mark the most important ideas in your study notes?		
Do you use sticky notes to mark texts and research books?		
Do you practise answering multiple-choice and written-response questions?		
Do you ask your teacher for help when you need it?		
Are you maintaining a healthy diet and sleep routine?		
Are you participating in regular physical activity?		

Related Issue 1

Should Ideology Be the Foundation of Identity?

RELATED ISSUE 1

Table of Correlations		
Specific Outcome	**Practice Questions**	**Unit Test Questions**
By the end of this course, students will:		
12.1 *Students will explore the relationship between identity and ideology*		
12.1.3 *explore factors that may influence individual and collective beliefs and values*	5, 7, 11	2
12.1.4 *examine historic and contemporary expressions of individualism and collectivism*	4, 12	10, 13
12.1.5 *examine the characteristics of ideology*	1	1, 14
12.1.6 *explore themes of ideologies*	6, 8	3, 6, 18
12.1.7 *analyze individualism as a foundation of ideology*	3, 9, 10, 13	4, 8, 12, 20, 22, 23
12.1.8 *analyze collectivism as a foundation of ideology*	2	5, 9, 15, 16, 17, 19, 21
12.1.9 *analyze the dynamic between individualism and common good in contemporary societies*	9, 14, 15	7, 11
12.1.10 *evaluate the extent to which personal identity should be shaped by ideologies*		24

RELATED ISSUE 1: SHOULD IDEOLOGY BE THE FOUNDATION OF IDENTITY?

12.1.3   Explore factors that may influence individual and collective beliefs and values

12.1.4   Examine historic and contemporary expressions of individualism and collectivism

12.1.5   Examine the characteristics of ideology

12.1.6   Explore themes of ideologies

THE FOUNDATION OF IDENTITY

IDEOLOGY

An ideology is a collection of ideas and beliefs, generally relating to politics and society. Ideologies can be embraced by individuals and societies, and, to at least some extent, make up part of their identities. Certain ideologies—, such as individualism, collectivism, liberalism, and totalitarianism, —are important parts of history and help shape who people are, as individuals, living within a larger society.

Ideologies include specific beliefs about various societal factors.

- Religion—people's systems of belief regarding the nature of the universe and their place in it.

- Relationship to the land—the way in which people extract resources from the environment.

- Spirituality—people's personal sense of the nature of the universe and their place in it.

- Language—the way in which people use words to communicate with one another.

- Media—the way in which people spread information through society.

- Culture - people's patterns of behaviour and modes of expression.

- Gender—people's views about the roles of men and women.

- Environment - the area in which people live.

Because ideologies incorporate so many beliefs about so many different societal factors, they affect the way in which people see the world. Thus, people with differing ideologies will likely hold different views of history, human nature, the structure of society, and what the future will hold.

Ideologies often emphasize a particular theme. For example, a person with a nationalist ideology will assess societal factors according to the way in which they impact his or her nation—the political and geographical area in which he or she lives. Another person might believe that social class is the most important theme and support a particular social class or class system. Still another person might be strongly religious or protective of the environment, and this person will base his or her ideologies on those themes.

Some ideologies are individualist; that is, they emphasize the importance of the individual in society. Others are collectivist—they emphasize the importance of the community. Still others are mixed: in practice, even strongly individualistic societies incorporate some collectivism (and vice versa).

12.1.7   Analyze individualism as a foundation of ideology

THE CHARACTERISTICS OF INDIVIDUALISM

Individualism is characterized by a lack of restraint on the freedom of individuals.
Government, for the most part, is not to interfere with the way in which individuals choose to conduct their lives. Thus, individualism is strongly linked with liberal ideology. It is important to note that the term "*liberal*" in this sense does not refer to the political ideology of the federal or provincial Liberal parties in Canada. Liberal ideologies are those that support individualism within the framework of politics and society. Most western democracies are liberal democracies, regardless of which political party forms the government.

Liberal societies guarantee certain rights and freedoms to their citizens - such as freedom of speech, freedom of association, and the right to vote. Citizens are free to pursue their own interests, even if they are not directly beneficial to society as a whole. The concept of self-interest is central to liberal economies. In short, the goverment does not intervene in a liberal economy unless it is to protect individuals from harm.

In a liberal society, no one is above the law This concept is known as the rule of law. Unlike the kings and aristocrats of the Middle Ages, the rulers in liberal democracies such as the prime minister and the members of Parliament) obey the same laws as the rest of the nation's citizens.
The law exists to protect people and property from harm or abuse. In other words, citizens are not allowed to infringe on the rights of others. Citizens are not free to hurt others, take their goods, or enter their homes uninvited.

Citizens in liberal societies may own private property. They are free to use, sell, keep, give away, or consume what they own as they choose, provided they do not break the law in doing so. Unless they are invited to do so, other people are not legally allowed to take, use, or trespass upon the private property of another.

12.1.8   analyse collectivism as a foundation of ideology

THE CHARACTERISTICS OF COLLECTIVISM

Collectivist societies restrict the freedom of individuals when necessary for the good of the society as a whole. Where individualism tends to correlate strongly with liberalism, collectivism has encompassed a wide variety of ideologies and societies: communism, fascism, agricultural cooperatives, some religious communities, etc. Therefore,identifying a specific ideological association for collectivism is difficult. There are, however, characteristics common to collectivist ideologies.

The central idea of collectivism is that people work together to achieve a common goal.
People in a collectivist society are expected to sacrifice certain personal freedoms (voluntarily or involuntarily) in pursuit of the goal. In return, they share in the rewards once the goal has been achieved.

This concept—communal sharing of rewards or benefits—leads to economic equality.
Because people are pursuing a common interest, they achieve a common profit from their labour. In an economically free society, people succeed or fail according to their own personal endeavours, market forces, or just plain luck. This can result in inequality, in which some people are rich and some are poor. A collective economy eliminates this inequality—individuals within the collective are not richer or poorer than their fellow citizens.

Under collectivism, people are generally expected to adhere to a set of social and political views held in common by the collective. People who deviate from these views come under pressure to adopt the collective view. This is achieved through social pressure, or, in totalitarian collectives, enforced by the state. The collective view is important to the success of the collective as a whole, because it helps reinforce the community and keeps people working toward the common goal.

Finally, in collectivist societies, there is no real private property. Material goods are distributed among the citizens according to need. Land, factories, and other means of production are owned by the collective and used to achieve the collective's goals.

12.1.9   Analyze the dynamic between individualism and common good in contemporary societies

INDIVIDUALISM AND THE COMMON GOOD

Modern societies incorporate elements of both individualism and collectivism, according to their dominant ideologies. In Canada, which is a liberal democracy, individual liberties are provided for while preserving the common good. In other words, people's freedoms are protected by law—freedom of speech, freedom of the press, and other core liberal-democratic values are guaranteed in the Constitution of Canada. Canadian citizens may own private property, they have an elected government, and that government must obey the rule of law.

At the same time, Canada, like other Western democracies, has government programs designed to assist those who, for whatever reason, are unable to afford the basic necessities of life. Canadians pay taxes, which are used, in part, to fund these social programs. This redistribution of wealth is characteristic of collectivism.

The attempt here is to find a balance between individualism and collectivism that will provide the greatest benefit for the greatest number of people—this is the concept of the common good. In other words, while people are free to pursue their own interests, they have certain obligations to their communities in order to achieve the common good. Thus, people cannot refuse to obey the law, to pay taxes, or to serve on juries when asked. To do so would be to undermine society and, therefore, the common good.

12.1.10   Evaluate the extent to which personal identity should be shaped by ideologies

IDEOLOGY AND THE INDIVIDUAL

The relationship between the individual and ideology is complex. In general, people follow a particular ideology because it makes sense to them. It fits with the way in which they view themselves and the world. At the same time, people are shaped by their ideologies to some extent. Most people who grow up in a liberal democracy will inevitably adopt some form of liberal-democratic ideology and instinctively reject ideas that arise from contrary ideologies.

The most important thing to keep in mind is that ideology is a choice. Although people are seldom conscious of the countless ways in which their ideologies influence them, people can work on understanding how they do so and just how much they form part of people's identities. There is nothing inherently wrong with identifying strongly with a particular ideology. The point here is to be aware of how ideologies affect the choices people make and their view of the world.

PRACTICE QUESTIONS—RELATED ISSUE 1

1. Liberalism is **most strongly** linked with which of the following ideologies?

   A. Nationalism

   B. Collectivism

   C. Individualism

   D. Totalitarianism

2. In a collectivist society, individuals have economic

   A. power

   B. equality

   C. freedom

   D. opportunity

3. The principle of the rule of law means that

   A. no one is above the law

   B. citizens must obey the law

   C. the government can make new laws

   D. the law courts judge the validity of laws

4. Which of the following attributes is **not** a factor in Canada being a liberal democracy?

   A. Periodic elections

   B. A capitalist economy

   C. A strong Liberal party

   D. The Constitution of Canada

Four people at four different protest rallies were asked why they felt the need to take part in the protest.

Speaker I

This forest has been here for centuries, and it is home to countless species of plants and animals. Now LumberCo wants to turn these majestic trees into toilet paper and tissue! It is up to citizens like you and me to stop these companies from destroying Canada's natural heritage.

—Natasha, university student

Speaker II

I am sick and tired of having the government interfering in radio, television, and the arts. Who are they to decide what citizens should or should not be exposed to? If I paint a picture, some people might find it offensive, but so what? If you don't like it, don't look at it! People should be free to express themselves.

—Michael, graphic designer

Speaker III

Until the owners of this company start treating their employees better, we are on strike. It is our hard work that made them rich in the first place. The least they could do is give us a decent wage and benefits. Instead, they treat us like disposable parts. Well, they are going to learn that without the right parts, the machine breaks down.

—Corey, electromechanical equipment assembler

Speaker IV

It is absolutely shocking, in this day and age, that women still do not receive equal treatment to men in the workplace. Canada has pay equality legislation, but if you look at the statistics, there is still a big wage gap. If a woman does the same work as a man, she should receive the same pay. Employers and provincial governments need to wake up—this is the 21st century!

—Shirin, lawyer

5. Which speaker has based his or her protest on the societal factor of gender?

   A. Speaker I

   B. Speaker II

   C. Speaker III

   D. Speaker IV

6. Which speaker adheres **most closely** to liberal ideology?

   A. Speaker I

   B. Speaker II

   C. Speaker III

   D. Speaker IV

7. Which speaker adheres **most closely** to collectivist ideology?

   A. Speaker I

   B. Speaker II

   C. Speaker III

   D. Speaker IV

8. Speaker I is concerned about the way in which a company is extracting resources from the environment. Which societal factor does this reflect?

   A. Private land usage

   B. Relationship to the land

   C. Sustainable development

   D. Environmental stewardship

9. Which two speakers **most likely** hold compatible viewpoints?

   A. Speakers I and II

   B. Speakers I and III

   C. Speakers II and IV

   D. Speakers III and IV

10. Which of the following ideas does not fit with an individualist ideology?

    A. Free speech

    B. Voting rights

    C. Public property

    D. Private property

Use the following information to answer the next question.

- Use of sentencing circles
- Candidates with no political party affiliation
- Society being more important than the individual

11. The given ideas and actions are best matched with which philosophy?

    A. Postmodernism

    B. Classis liberalism

    C. Modern liberalism

    D. Aboriginal collective thought

Use the following information to answer the next question.

> • *An Inconvenient Truth* by Al Gore
> • *Silent Spring* by Rachel Carlson
> • The Kyoto Accord

12. From the perspective of a classical liberal economist, the ideas contained in the given documents would result in

    A. an economic boom

    B. economic hardship

    C. an environmental disaster

    D. environmental and economic success

13. An individual would be least likely to self-identify ideologically as

    A. liberal

    B. an extremist

    C. conservative

    D. an environmentalist

Use the following information to answer the next question.

> • French language rights
> • Affirmative action
> • Aboriginal rights

14. The given rights and actions are best described as

    A. perceived rights

    B economic rights

    C. collective rights

    D. individual rights

15. Environmental concerns are often in opposition to

    A. socialism

    B. capitalism

    C. collectivism

    D. individualism

ANSWERS AND SOLUTIONS—PRACTICE QUESTIONS

1. C	4. C	7. C	10. C	13. B
2. B	5. D	8. B	11. D	14. C
3. A	6. B	9. D	12. B	15. B

1. C

Liberalism, with its emphasis on individual liberties, is strongly linked with individualism, which opposes any limit on an individual's choices or actions.

Nationalism can exist as part of any nation. Liberalism is not a collectivist ideology, since collectivism restricts individual liberties. Liberalism is in complete opposition to totalitarianism, in which the rights and freedoms of individuals are suppressed by the state.

2. B

In a collectivist society, citizens benefit equally from the work of the collective.

Economic power depends on the success of the collective, rather than the individual. Economic freedom and opportunity are inherent to individualist, free market economies.

3. A

According to the rule of law, no one is above the law, including the country's political and social elite.

Even in countries that do not have the rule of law, the government makes laws that citizens must obey. In liberal democracies, law courts such as the Supreme Court of Canada can rule on the validity of a law only if it violates the Constitution (including the rule of law).

4. C

The Liberal Party of Canada has nothing to do with Canada's status as a liberal democracy. Canada is just as much a liberal democracy under Conservative rule as it is under Liberal rule.

5. D

As a societal factor, gender refers to a society's views of the roles of men and women. Speaker IV is primarily concerned with the lack of pay equality between men and women in similar roles. Therefore, this speaker is concerned with gender.

6. B

Speaker II advocates freedom of expression. Freedom of expression is part of liberal ideology, but most liberal governments exercise at least some control in order to protect the public from libellous, slanderous, or obscene works.

7. C

Speaker III talks about going on strike— and is likely part of a union. A union is a collectivist organization created to protect and promote worker's rights. Therefore, Speaker III is, in part, an adherent of collectivist ideology.

8. B

Relationship to the land is the societal factor concerned with the extraction of resources.

The other given options are all specific ideological stances on relationship to the land.

9. D

Speakers III and IV are both concerned with what they see as a lack of fairness in the workplace. Therefore, they are pursuing similar goals, albeit in different fashions.

10. C

Individualists prefer a lack of restraint on the freedom of individuals. Even if public property is beneficial to the society as a whole, individualists prefer private ownership.

11. D.

Using sentencing circles, having candidates with no political party affiliation, and viewing society as more important than the individual are all ideas and actions that are best matched with aboriginal collective thought.

12. B

A classical liberal economist would view the ideas from *An Inconvenient Truth, Silent Spring,* and the Kyoto Accord as creating economic hardship for most of the world, because all three of these documents promote environmentalism at a huge cost to the economy.

Most governments are trying to find a balance between improving the environment and maintaining a strong economy.

13. B.

Extremist is a label that individuals are not likely to use to describe themselves. It is a term usually used to describe others, and it is usually stated in a negative way.

Extremism is generally an ideology outside the spectrum of any mainstream ideology. It often involves tactics and actions that are considered unacceptable morally, socially, and legally. However it is possible, for ideas that were previously believed to be extremist to become mainstream or conventional in a different time, such as women's rights and desegregation.

14. C

French language rights, affirmative action, and aboriginal rights are all types of collective rights.

15. B

Environmental concerns and movements are often in opposition to capitalism.

UNIT TEST—RELATED ISSUE 1

1. What is an ideology?

   A. A political stance

   B. An economic theory

   C. A collection of ideas and beliefs

   D. A society's dominant cultural practices

2. In a society, the purpose of the media is to

   A. provide facts

   B. spread information

   C. report current events

   D. offer unbiased reporting

Use the following information to answer the next four questions.

A magazine writer wants to write an article on Canadian identity. The writer goes to a busy downtown transit stop and asks passersby for their opinions on Canadian society.

Speaker I

 We Canadians care for our fellow citizens. If someone is sick, injured, poor, or unemployed, the government has programs in place to take care of them. And isn't it the government's job to look after its citizens? Imagine living in the United States, where medical bills can leave people deeply in debt. Living in Canada is way better.

—Aiden, computer technician

Speaker II

 When I came to Canada, I did not own much more than the clothes I was wearing. But I worked hard and saved money until I could afford to open my own restaurant. Now look at me—three restaurants, a nice house, and I can afford to send my kids to university. That never could have happened in the country I used to live in. Coming to Canada was the best choice I have ever made.

—Amy, restaurant owner

Speaker III

 I travel a lot, and everywhere I go, people are friendly when they find out that I am a Canadian. Canada is respected around the world for its fairness, tolerance, and commitment to peace and freedom. We are everyone's friend, and it makes me proud to be Canadian.

—Ibrahim, business executive

Speaker IV

 Canada is the best! We have the best food, the best sports, the best music, the best television shows, and the best people. Our country has some of the most beautiful wilderness areas in the world. We have tons of festivals and art shows, so there is always lots of stuff to do. I would never want to live anywhere else.

—Katja, pharmacist

3. Speaker III would **most likely** oppose which of the following government initiatives?

    A. Deploying peacekeeping forces to war-torn areas

    B. Erecting a monument honouring Second World War veterans

    C. Imposing trade sanctions against countries that violate human rights

    D. Condemning developing nations for using environmentally unsafe practices

4. Which speaker **most strongly** displays individualist ideology?

    A. Speaker I

    B. Speaker II

    C. Speaker III

    D. Speaker IV

5. Which speaker **most strongly** displays collectivist ideology?

    A. Speaker I

    B. Speaker II

    C. Speaker III

    D. Speaker IV

6. All four speakers display elements of which ideology?

    A. Liberalism

    B. Nationalism

    C. Internationalism

    D. Environmentalism

7. A strongly liberal government would **most likely** intervene in the economy in order to perform which of the following actions?

    A. Set standards for food safety

    B. Impose minimum wage laws

    C. Support a failing business during a recession

    D. Prevent a lumber company from clear-cutting a forest

8. In liberal societies, citizens are expected to

    A. pursue their own interests

    B. work for the benefit of others

    C. adhere to a common ideology

    D. put the interests of the state before their own

9. In a collectivist society, individuals work for the good of
   A. the state
   B. themselves
   C. the community
   D. the environment

10. What type of government does Canada have?
    A. A federal republic
    B. A liberal democracy
    C. An absolute monarchy
    D. An enlightened autocracy

11. The concept of providing the greatest benefit to the greatest number of people is known as the
    A. common goal
    B. common good
    C. collective goal
    D. collective good

12. Under liberal economies, individuals have equality of
    A. status
    B. power
    C. opportunity
    D. remuneration

13. In general, the economies of Western democracies are
    A. mixed
    B. totalitarian
    C. collectivist
    D. individualist

Use the following information to answer the next four questions.

Four workers in four different factories were asked what motivated them in their jobs.

Speaker I

I am proud to work here because I know that I am helping my country. If our nation is to become great, every citizen must contribute. Those who cannot or will not contribute are justly punished; a strong society cannot afford to support the weak.

Speaker II

When I first started working here, my labour only profited the factory's owners. Now, it is the workers who own and operate the factory, and it is the workers who profit. The goods I make will help my fellow citizens. With every citizen working together, no one will lack for anything.

Speaker III

I like working as part of a community. We do not have to rely on outsiders to survive. We are totally self-sufficient. My coworkers are also my family. I know I can rely on them, just as they can rely on me.

Speaker IV

I work hard so that I can provide for myself and my family. I earn enough here that we can live comfortably. And who knows? If I work hard enough, I may earn a promotion and get a higher salary.

14. Which speaker identifies **most strongly** with the liberal ideology?

    A. Speaker I

    B. Speaker II

    C. Speaker III

    D. Speaker IV

15. Which speakers **most likely** work in collectivist societies?

    A. Speakers I and II

    B. Speakers I and IV

    C. Speakers II and III

    D. Speakers II and IV

16. Which speaker adheres to a totalitarian ideology?

    A. Speaker I

    B. Speaker II

    C. Speaker III

    D. Speaker IV

17. If Speaker III got angry and refused to work, he or she would **most likely** be
    A. fired and replaced.

    B. executed as a traitor.

    C. imprisoned as a dissident.

    D. expelled from the community.

18. Nationalism, environmentalism, and racism have which of the following traits in common?
    A. They all promote individualism.

    B. They are all historically significant.

    C. They all emphasize a specific theme.

    D. They are all based on distinct geographical areas.

19. In collectivist societies, goods are distributed according to
    A. need

    B. contribution

    C. personal wealth

    D. the hierarchy of professions

Use the following information to answer the next two questions.

George is a farmer. He is ploughing his field when his plough suddenly breaks. He does not have a spare. He knows his neighbour is away for a day or two so he goes to his neighbour's shed, takes the plough, and finishes his work. He then returns the plough to his neighbour's shed.

20. In an individualist society, would the farmer's actions be acceptable? Explain.

_____

_____

_____

_____

21. In a collectivist society, would the farmer's actions be acceptable? Explain.

_____

_____

_____

_____

22. What is the **main** characteristic of individualist societies?

_____

_____

_____

_____

23. What is the role of the law in a liberal society?

_____

_____

_____

_____

24. In collectivist societies, why is it important for individuals to adhere to the social and political views of the collective?

_____

_____

_____

_____

ANSWERS AND SOLUTIONS—UNIT TEST

1.	C	7.	A	13.	A	19.	A
2.	B	8.	A	14.	D	20.	See solution
3.	D	9.	C	15.	C	21.	See solution
4.	B	10.	B	16.	A	22.	See solution
5.	A	11.	B	17.	D	23.	See solution
6.	B	12.	C	18.	C	24.	See solution

1. C

An ideology is a collection of ideas and beliefs about society.

Politics, economics, and culture all form part of an ideology, along with a number of other societal factors and themes.

2. B

The role of the media (newspapers, radio, television, the Internet, etc.) is to spread information within a society.

Even in a liberal democracy, the media is not always a factual or unbiased source of information. It is important to note here that, in this context, the term *media* does not refer only to journalism, but to any means of spreading information. Therefore, the term *media* in this sense might include talk shows, Internet blogs, or celebrity gossip magazines.

3. D

Speaker III is primarily concerned with Canada's international reputation. Although environmental protection is desirable, condemning developing nations may harm Canada's reputation.

Speaker III would likely support anything that demonstrates Canada's commitment to peace and freedom.

4. B

Speaker II is an entrepreneur who has benefited from Canada's liberal economy. Free market economies are inherent to the individualist ideology.

5. A

Speaker I strongly supports social welfare programs. This sort of redistribution of wealth is part of the collectivist ideology.

6. B

All four speakers express nationalist sentiment—that their nation is somehow special or superior to other nations.

Liberal ideology (support for individual freedoms) is largely ignored by most of the speakers. Only Speaker III displays internationalist sentiment. None of the speakers display environmentalist sentiment.

7. A

A liberal government would intervene to protect people from unsafe food products. In a liberal society, it is not acceptable to endanger citizens.

In the case of minimum wage laws, a strongly liberal government would allow the labour market to regulate itself. A liberal government would also let free market forces take their course, even if it meant a business might fail. Finally, a liberal government would not interfere with the property rights of whoever owned the land on which the forest grew.

8. **A**

   Citizens in liberal societies are expected to act in their own interests, both politically and economically. This is particularly essential to the workings of the free market economy. This does not mean that people in liberal societies are greedy or selfish. By acting in their own interests, they benefit society as a whole.

9. **C**

   The community is the most important part of collectivist societies. Individuals are expected to work for the benefit of everyone in the community, not just themselves.

   Ideally, the state is not an important part of a collectivist society, although totalitarian-collectivist societies do exist. Whether or not individuals work for the good of the environment depends on the collective in question.

10. **B**

    Canada, like most Western democracies, is a liberal democracy.

    Federal republics, such as the United States, are democracies without a monarch as the head of state; Canada still technically pays allegiance to the British monarch. Absolute monarchies and enlightened autocracies are both illiberal forms of government, in which political power stems from a single ruler.

11. **B**

    The common good is an important societal concept in both individualist and collectivist societies. Most non-totalitarian societies seek to provide the greatest good to the greatest number of people, within their particular ideology.

12. **C**

    In theory, everyone in a liberal, free market economy has the opportunity to grow wealthy.

    Equality of status, power, and remuneration (pay) are generally found in collectivist societies.

13. **A**

    Mixed economies are those that employ both individualist and collectivist elements. Western democracies have capitalist (free market) economies, but they also employ tax revenue to fund social welfare programs.

14. **D**

    Speaker IV is primarily concerned with the personal compensation received from work. Thus, the speaker is motivated by self-interest and functions in a capitalist economy—both hallmarks of the liberal ideology.

15. **C**

    Speakers II and III work in collectivist societies. Speaker II works in a large-scale collective—a communist or socialist nation. Speaker III works in a smaller, community-based collective.

    Speaker I works in a totalitarian society, and that society is obviously not concerned for the welfare of its citizens. Speaker IV works in a liberal society, so he personally benefits from his labour.

16. A

Speaker I is solely concerned with the power of the nation-state and cares little for the welfare of his fellow citizens. These are characteristics of totalitarian ideology.

17. D

In small-scale collectives or communes, it is important for all members to work together. If a member chooses not to work with the rest of the collective, he or she cannot remain as part of the community. By refusing to work, Speaker III would be disrupting the accord that keeps the community together.

18. C

Nationalism, environmentalism, and racism are ideologies based on a particular theme.

None of the ideologies listed promote individualism; in most cases, the reverse is true. Historical significance is a value judgment. For example, one might see the environmentalist movement as too new to have attained historical significance. Finally, while nationalism is based on a distinct region, environmentalism and racism are not. Environmentalism can have local concerns such as preventing pollution in a specific area but often has a more global focus like ozone depletion and climate change).

19. A

In collectivist societies, goods go to the people who need them most.

Contribution is irrelevant; people are expected to contribute what they can according to their individual abilities. Personal wealth does not exist in collectivist societies. Finally, professions are not ranked in collectivist societies. For example, a doctor does not receive greater compensation than a factory worker.

20.

The farmer's actions would not be acceptable in an individualist society. Laws in individualist societies protect private property. The farmer has no right to enter his neighbour's shed and borrow the plough unless he has obtained his neighbour's permission beforehand. Otherwise, he has broken the law.

21.

The farmer's actions would be acceptable in a collectivist society. In a collective, there is no private property. The neighbour's plough and shed are public property, as is the farmer's land. Since the farmer is acting in the best interests of the community, his actions are perfectly acceptable.

22.

Individualism is characterized by a lack of restraint on the freedom of individuals.

23.

In a liberal society, the law exists to protect people and property from harm or abuse.

24.

The collective view helps to reinforce a sense of community and keeps people working toward the common goal.

Related Issue 2

To What Extent Is Resistance to Liberalism Justified?

RELATED ISSUE 2

Table of Correlations

Specific Outcome		Practice Questions	Unit Test Questions
By the end of this course, students will:			
12.2	*Students will assess impacts of, and reactions to, principles of liberalism*		
12.2.5	examine the relationship between the principles of liberalism and the origins of classical liberal thought	1, 2, 27	1, 2, 3, 5
12.2.6	analyze the impacts of classical liberal thought on 19th century society	3, 4, 5, 6, 7, 8, 9	4, 6, 8, 26
12.2.7	analyze ideologies that developed in response to classical liberalism	10, 11, 12, 26	7, 9, 10
12.2.8	analyze the evolution of modern liberalism as a response to classical liberalism	13, 14, 15, 28	11, 12
12.2.9	evaluate ideological systems that rejected principles of liberalism	16, 17, 18, 19, 20, 21	13, 14, 15, 16, 17
12.2.10	analyze how ideological conflict shaped international relations after the Second World War	22, 23, 24, 32, 33, 34	18, 19, 20, 21, 22, 23, 24, 27
12.2.12	analyze analyze the extent to which modern liberalism is challenged by alternative thought	25, 29, 30, 31	25

RELATED ISSUE 2: TO WHAT EXTENT IS RESISTANCE TO LIBERALISM JUSTIFIED?

12.2.5 Examine the relationship between the principles of liberalism and the origins of classical liberal thought

12.2.6 Analyze the impacts of classical liberal thought on 19th century society

THE ROOTS OF CLASSICAL LIBERALISM

Classical liberalism finds its roots in the Age of Enlightenment, which followed the Renaissance period in Europe. The arts continued to flourish in Europe, nations were growing wealthy with goods from the New World, contact with foreign cultures was increasing, and a new spirit of scientific inquiry was growing among European intellectuals. The near-absolute authority of the Catholic Church had been severely curtailed by the Protestant Reformation, and people increasingly wondered about the place of the individual in society.

As a result, the Enlightenment was fertile ground for the development of new political and social inquiry. The roots of this inquiry were the political systems of the classical era: the democracy of ancient Athens and the pre-imperial Roman republic. It was nurtured by a variety of liberal thinkers: Locke, Rousseau, Smith, Montesquieu, and many others.

Baron de Montesquieu (1689–1755)

Charles de Secondat, Baron de Montesquieu, was a French aristocrat and political satirist who opposed the absolute monarchy in France. He believed people should be equal and the government should be accountable to the citizenry. The way to do this, according to Montesquieu, was to establish a democracy, in which it was important for every citizen to be an active participant in government.

Montesquieu's most important contribution to liberal ideology was the idea of the separation of powers into executive, legislative, and judicial branches. This idea is central to many modern democracies, including Canada and the United States. The separation of powers prevents any particular branch from accumulating too much power.

SOCIAL CONTRACT THEORY

As political thought developed during the Enlightenment, philosophers began to ask certain questions. What induces people to form states and become part of larger societies? What would life be like in the absence of the state? What is the relationship of individuals to the state? These questions all led to social contract theory. The social order is, in effect, a contract between the individual and the state.

Thomas Hobbes (1588–1679)

The experiences in Hobbes' life taught him that human beings, although not evil, were selfish by nature. Thus, in the absence of the state, this selfishness would lead people to harm one another. In *Leviathan*, Hobbes asserts that human beings voluntarily surrender their individual freedoms to the state in order to receive the state's protection. Hobbes' social contract implies that the state must assure the security of the citizens, and the citizens, in turn, surrender themselves to the authority of the state.

John Locke (1632–1704)

Locke was among the most influential political philosophers of the Enlightenment. His ideas influenced several other philosophers, as well as the framers of the United States Constitution and the French revolutionaries' *Declaration of the Rights of Man and of the Citizen*. He opposed the absolute authority of the state and the church; he felt that individuals should rely on themselves to make important decisions, rather than having decisions imposed on them.

Locke's idea of the social contract, as laid out in his *Two Treatises of Government*, is far more liberal than that of Hobbes. Locke believed that security and social order are important as a means to allow people to accumulate and protect their private property. In this way, people can retain an amount of sovereignty over themselves. In order to preserve this sovereignty, it is important that the government be accountable to the citizens.

Jean-Jacques Rousseau (1712–1778)

Rousseau's idea of the social contract differs markedly from both Hobbes and Locke. Unlike Hobbes, Rousseau believed that human beings are naturally good, compassionate, and free. He also believed that human beings could return to this natural state by reclaiming their own sovereignty.

Rousseau, unlike Locke, believed in direct democracy: that every citizen should have a voice in the government and in the creation of laws (Locke supported representative democracy). This would mean that laws would not restrict people's freedoms, but express them, since the will of the people determined the shape of the law.

THE APPLICATION OF CLASSICAL LIBERALISM

As people became increasingly aware of classical liberal theories, they sought to move from theory to practice. European governments were, for the most part, feudalist monarchies; the idea that a commoner could have a voice in the government was revolutionary. Indeed, liberal thought sparked two revolutions and brought the downfall of the economic system of the time.

Classical Liberal Economics: Adam Smith (1723–1790)

Smith was a Scottish philosopher who was opposed to the mercantile economic system of his day. Mercantilism operates under the assumption that precious metals (gold and silver) are the real measure of a nation's wealth, and that trade between nations always results in a winner and a loser. Mercantile governments freely intervened in the economy of their countries to maximize exports and minimize imports. By the 18th century, the flaws of the mercantile system were apparent. Large, government-sponsored monopolies had a stranglehold on trade, the nations of Europe were in near-constant conflict, and conditions for the working class were appalling.

In 1776, Adam Smith published *An Inquiry into the Nature and Causes of the Wealth of Nations* (generally known as *The Wealth of Nations*). This revolutionary book is the foundation of modern economics. In *The Wealth of Nations*, Smith overturns many of the key assumptions that underlie mercantilism and provides a framework for a new conception of wealth and economic prosperity.

Smith points out that trade does not have to be a competition among nations. In fact, trade can be mutually beneficial. For example, if one nation has surplus cloth but needs iron, and another nation has surplus iron but needs cloth, then the trade will benefit both nations. In other words, wealth is not based on gold and silver, but on commodities.

The value of a commodity, according to Smith, is only partially based on its scarcity or demand. The other, more important factor is the labour required to obtain, produce, and transport the commodity. Smith believed that labour was the real value behind commodities. Therefore, a person's labour does not only benefit that person (in the form of wages), but the economy as a whole.

Capitalism: Laissez-Faire Economics

Smith also recognized that people tended to act in their own interests, but this was not necessarily a bad thing. Indeed, an individual's self-interest would result in a host of benefits. For example, a baker makes bread in order to sell it for a profit. The flour required for the baking must be purchased from a miller, who is likewise acting in his own interest. Thus, they both profit: the miller sells flour, and the baker sells bread. Likewise, the customer who purchases the bread is not interested in the baker's profit, but in obtaining food. Again, both parties benefit: the baker profits, and the customer has food.

Smith refers to these unintended benefits of self-interest as the "invisible hand," which is one of the better-known points in *The Wealth of Nations*. The invisible hand works for the benefit of all, and it works just fine without government interference. Smith strongly advocated the cessation of government interference in the economy, since the market would regulate itself though the actions of the invisible hand. This practice—minimal government interference in the economy—is called laissez-faire economics. *Laissez-faire* is a French term that approximately translates to, "leave it alone."

This is not to say that Smith saw no role for the government in the economy. He was fully aware of the dehumanizing effect that tedious labour could have on the working class, and believed governments needed to intervene for the well-being of society. He was also in favour of progressive taxation; that is, that the wealthiest classes should pay a higher proportion of their income in taxes than the working classes. Because labour is an important source of value, Smith felt it was important that the government be able to maintain a certain basic level of sustenance and education.

The American Revolution and the Aboriginal Contribution

The British colonies in America grew increasingly dissatisfied with their government during the Enlightenment. The autocratic treatment they received, coupled with a new zeal for liberalism, led the Americans to rise up against British rule and establish the world's first liberal-democratic government. The framers of the United States Constitution relied on the ideals of liberal philosophers such as Locke and Montesquieu, as well as on the example of the Haudenosaunee Confederacy.

The Haudenosaunee are an aboriginal people who lived near the Great Lakes; the nations of the confederacy lived under the Great Law of Peace. This law united the Haudenosaunee people and contained many of the rights and freedoms that now form the core of modern liberalism. The Great Law of Peace also made women active participants in government—something that Europe and its colonies would not do until much later.

The French Revolution

The Age of Enlightenment came to a close with the French Revolution. The revolutionaries were initially motivated by several factors: resentment of the French king's autocratic rule, widespread liberal sentiment in France, and the success of the American Revolution. The French Revolution succeeded in toppling Louis XVI from the throne, but did not result in a stable liberal government. The victorious revolutionaries soon began to develop factions that vied for control of the government. The result was years of chaos, terror, and the destruction of property.

The Industrial Revolution

As industrialism took hold, workers flocked to cities to get jobs in factories. These workers were routinely exploited and had to work long hours in unsafe conditions for low wages. There was little, if any, protection of worker's rights. Because of the low wages, children and women often had to work to ensure the family's survival.

Industrialism itself was born out of liberal economic theory. Governments relaxed their grip on their economies and allowed greater freedom in the market. People realized it was commodities, not gold and silver, that were truly valuable. Because the value of a commodity is largely based on the labour required to produce it, people began to look for ways to lower labour costs. One of the ways to do this was to invent machines that could outperform human labourers. This first occurred in the textiles industry, and it was augmented by the introduction of steam power.

Predictably, this did not go over well with skilled artisans, who were unhappy about being replaced with the new machines. Soon, groups of angry workers began to break into factories to destroy equipment. These workers called themselves the Army of Redressers, but were more commonly known as Luddites. The government quickly passed laws making the destruction of machines punishable by death. In the end, the Luddites were not able to stem the tide of industrialism.

12.2.7   Analyze ideologies that developed in response to classical liberalism

12.2.8   Analyze the evolution of modern liberalism as a response to classical liberalism

THE TRANSITION TO MODERN LIBERALISM

Classical liberalism led to a stable and successful government in the United States, but in many ways, it was a failure. Classical liberal economics resulted in a volatile marketplace and the widespread exploitation of the new urban working class. Women were still very much considered to be second-class citizens or not citizens at all. Even staunch liberal philosophers gave little consideration to women's rights. The failure of the French Revolution had made rulers and citizens alike wary of liberalism, and liberalism encountered increasing resistance. Under these pressures, liberalism gradually evolved into liberalism as it is known today.

CONSERVATISM: EDMOND BURKE (1729–1797)

Burke was an Irish-born British member of Parliament in the mid- to late-18th century. He is now seen as the father of modern conservatism. Burke lived during the height of the Enlightenment, and he mistrusted the abstract and grandiose political theories of the day, especially social contract theory. Burke much preferred a concrete and clear political ideology- one based on strong principles, traditions, and morality.

In Burke's view, society's traditions (moral, religious, political, etc.) endure because they are valuable. Traditions create a shared sense of community, of right and wrong, of the past, and of the principles upon which the nation was founded. Therefore, societies should be wary of changing them, especially if the change is radical.

LABOUR MOVEMENTS

Conditions for the working class in the early modern era were poor—this would continue throughout the Industrial Revolution. The major social change brought about by the Industrial Revolution was the influx of people coming from the country to the city to look for work. Cities at the time were not equipped to handle the dramatic increase in population, so the working poor lived in small, packed dwellings. Sanitation was practically non-existent, and disease spread quickly in the cramped conditions. Cholera, smallpox, and typhoid all took a huge toll on the working poor. Industrial safety standards were also non-existent; industrial accidents and work-related illnesses such as pneumoconiosis from the inhalation of coal dust) were common.

With the industrial labourers living and working in close proximity to one another and sharing the same experiences, organization was perhaps inevitable. Although trade unions were frowned upon (and in many cases, illegal), the perseverance of the labour movement eventually resulted in better working conditions, restrictions on child labour, and increased political power. In Great Britain, for example, the franchise (right to vote) was extended three times in the latter half of the 19th century, and came to include the working class.

However, this did not come easily. In the early part of the century, a massive labour movement rallied behind the People's Charter, which comprised six points aimed at enfranchising all men over 21 and reforming the parliamentary system. The Chartists presented petitions with anywhere from 1 to 3 million signatures to Parliament. When these went unheard, the leaders threatened a general strike. Ultimately, when Parliament failed to hear the Chartists for the third and last time, most of the members joined the socialist movement.

THE RISE OF SOCIALISM

The poverty, poor working conditions, and other inequalities of industrialism also led to the development of socialist political and economic theory. Socialists believed that, rather than giving their labour to wealthy capitalists, workers should collectively own the means of production. Wealth should be distributed equitably among workers. The socialist movement of the nineteenth century quickly branched off into a number of offshoots. The most prominent of these was communism, which was largely developed by German philosophers Karl Marx and Friedrich Engels.

Communism was the most radical form of socialism. Marx and Engels predicted that the proletariat (working class) would violently seize the means of production from the bourgeoisie (wealthy class). First and foremost, communism is about the abolition of private property. Communists saw private property as the main source of the inequality between the socioeconomic classes. They also believed the government should have complete control over the economy; its role would be to distribute goods and assign labour according to the needs of the people.

MODERN LIBERALISM: JOHN STUART MILL (1806–1873)

Mill was a British philosopher whose best-known work, *On Liberty*, is one of the foundations of modern liberal thought. Mill believed that people should be free to do as they wished, unless it harmed another person. He believed free speech and freedom of the press were necessary to the function of liberal society. Mill also believed society could only develop through the free and uninhibited exchange and debate of various ideas.

However, Mill was not in favour of simple majority rule. He argued against the principle of the tyranny of the majority. This can occur in democratic societies in which the majority can legally oppress minorities. He believed that there was a social tyranny—the societal pressures that force citizens to conform to the mainstream. Therefore, liberal democracies must guard against either form of tyranny by remaining receptive to the views and needs of the minority. Mill was opposed to the treatment of women and non-Europeans as inferiors. He believed that, given the chance, they could contribute just as much to society as any European male.

WELFARE CAPITALISM AND THE WELFARE STATE

As the labour movement gathered strength, both governments and industrialists realized it was in their best interests to take heed of workers' complaints. This was a slow process, often punctuated by violent clashes, but it produced concrete results. Some industrialists voluntarily worked with their employees to resolve differences and provide them with housing, job security, and other benefits. Governments began to legislate worker's rights: minimum wage laws, maternity leave, pensions, medical insurance, and other such benefits that are now entrenched in most liberal democracies.

These laws form the core of the modern welfare statewhich is capitalist, but still provides for the welfare of citizens in need. The welfare state did not fully take shape until the Great Depression and the new theories of John Maynard Keynes.

MODERN LIBERAL ECONOMICS: JOHN MAYNARD KEYNES (1883–1946)

Adam Smith's labour-based free market economy was a cornerstone of classical liberalism, but it resulted in economies that fluctuated widely between periods of boom (prosperity) and bust (hardship). The greatest bust period occurred in the 1930s and is now known as the Great Depression.

Keynes, a British economist, proposed a system of government regulation designed to flatten the economic cycle. He suggested that during periods of recession, governments should spend more money on public works or social programs, while lowering taxes, since this would keep money circulating in the economy. During periods of inflation, governments should spend less money and increase taxes, since this would keep inflation in check and cool demand. Keynes' economic theory is called demand-side economics, because the government influences the demand aspect of the supply-demand dynamic.

Keynesian economics were at the core of President Franklin D. Roosevelt's New Deal. Under the New Deal, the United States government instituted a number of work projects (construction, tree-planting, and so forth) to provide jobless Americans with gainful employment. The New Deal also introduced stock-market regulation, bank deposit insurance, funding for the arts, and more. These became the foundation of the modern welfare state.

Although Keynesian economics helped some countries recover from the Depression, his theories were not fully implemented. Governments are popular when they increase spending on public works and lower taxes. But are less willing to risk unpopularity by raising taxes while cutting social programs. By failing to cut spending and increase taxes during inflationary periods, governments risk going into debt.

12.2.9   Evaluate ideological systems that rejected principles of liberalism

IDEOLOGICAL SYSTEMS THAT REJECTED PRINCIPLES OF LIBERALISM

SOVIET COMMUNISM

Communist ideology first took hold in Russia during the First World War. A popular revolution forced the Russian czar to abdicate in February of 1917. In October of the same year, the Bolsheviks, a party of hard-line Communists led by Vladimir Lenin, took control of the Russian government. They based their new government around collective units of workers, farmers, and soldiers called *soviets*. Thus, Russia became the heart of the Union of Soviet Socialist Republics (USSR), or the Soviet Union.

The new Communist regime withdrew from the First World War to concentrate on domestic matters, which largely consisted of a civil war against remnants of the czarist regime and other parties opposed to communism. In order to supply his army, Lenin instituted war communism: an instant transition to a command economy with the immediate abolition of private property. However, war communism proved both extremely unproductive and extremely unpopular. Industrial and agricultural production plummeted, and even staunch Bolshevik supporters protested against the measures taken.

Lenin was forced to introduce limited capitalism under the New Economic Policy (NEP). The NEP helped the Soviet Union recover from the ravages of the First World War and the Russian civil war. However, it also created a rich peasant class called the kulaks, which undermined the communist ideal of a classless society. When Josef Stalin took control of the Soviet Union, the NEP came to an end. In its place, Stalin implemented strict collectivization, persecuted the kulaks, and had the people work toward set production goals in industry and agriculture. These measures are known as the five-year plans.

Under Stalin, the country also became fully totalitarian. Political power was entirely in the hands of Stalin and the Communist bureaucracy. Necessary goods were not shared equally among the workers— but were distributed according to the requirements of the state and the five-year plans. This led to widespread famine, even in agriculturally rich areas like Ukraine. A great famine, now known as the *Holodomor*, occurred in Ukraine from 1932 to 1933, and it resulted in six million deaths.

The Soviet leadership also repressed any dissent or opposition through a series of arrests, imprisonments, and executions known as purges. By itself, the Great Purge of 1937 to 1938 accounted for nearly two million deaths. The purges were characterized by torture, forced confessions, show trials, executions, and disappearances. The secret police of the time—the NKVD—, were feared by peasants and politicians alike. Clearly, this was not the socialist paradise envisioned by the likes of Marx or Lenin.

NAZISM

The Treaty of Versailles that ended the First World War was harsh on the German people. Under the terms of the treaty, they were made to accept blame for the war and were forced to pay enormous reparations (monetary compensation) to their enemies. This was humiliating to the Germans, and it also destroyed the German economy. The ruling liberal-democratic government, known as the Weimar Republic, grew increasingly unstable and ineffectual.

All of these factors made liberalism unpopular in Germany. Some people longed for a return to the monarchy they had before the First World War. The German Kaiser was a relatively benign monarch, and had implemented several popular social programs. Others believed that the German people should adopt socialism. In short, almost all Germans resented the liberal governments that had imposed such harsh and unfair terms on them.

It was in this environment that Adolf Hitler and his National Socialist German Workers' Party (Nazis) flourished. The Nazis exploited people's frustration with the Treaty of Versailles and the Weimar Republic, and the Nazis soon became popular. Behind the scenes, the Nazis also used strong-arm tactics to intimidate political rivals. The paramilitary arm of the Nazi party was the *Sturmabteilung* (SA), which literally means "assault detachment." Ironically, part of Hitler's popularity came from his promise to quell the chaos and lawlessness in the streets, much of which was caused by the SA.

Eventually, the Nazis were able to gain control of the Reichstag, Germany's parliament, and dismantle its liberal-democratic elements. A fire at the Reichstag gave Hitler an excuse to declare a state of emergency, and, as chancellor, give himself absolute authority over Germany.

The Nazi regime touted the German people as the "master race" and claimed they were naturally superior to all other peoples. The Nazis attempted to purge what they considered weaknesses from the race by killing or sterilizing people who were disabled, mentally ill, handicapped, homosexual, or carriers of hereditary illnesses. This culminated in a policy called *Aktion T4*, which resulted in the execution of over 70 000 people.

Many racial groups, particularly Jews, Romani, and Slavs, were tagged as *"untermenchen"*, which literally means "subhumans". In particular Jews, had lived under a long and sad tradition of anti-Semitism throughout Europe. On their rise to power, the Nazis blamed the Jews for the problems plaguing Germany. Their attacks on the Jewish people grew ever more violent. On November 9, 1938, a massive anti-Jewish pogrom resulted in attacks on Jews, which included destruction of their homes, businesses, and places of worship as well as the arrest and internment of tens of thousands of Jewish people.

The Nazis also moved to restore national pride by regaining military strength. This went against the terms of the Treaty of Versailles. However, the war-weary nations of Europe were unwilling to enforce those terms, even when Hitler moved to seize Austria and the German-speaking portion of Czechoslovakia—the Sudetenland. Eventually, when Germany invaded Poland in September 1939, France and Britain realized that they had to go to war.

During the war, the Nazis aggressively pursued their campaign against those they deemed to be "lesser races." Millions were herded into concentration camps, while many more were forced to live in ghettos (racially-segregated neighbourhoods). The Nazis then moved to eliminate them. Inmates at the concentration camps were starved or worked to death. The *Schutzstaffel* (SS), which literally means "protection squad," oversaw much of this activity. They established special task forces called *Einsatzgruppen* to operate behind the lines of battle; the *Einsatzgruppen* organized mass executions of Jews, politicians, intellectuals, rebels, and other perceived enemies of the Third Reich.

Eventually, the SS created the notorious extermination camps. These places designed specifically for the mass slaughter of human beings. The most notorious of these is Auschwitz in Poland; indeed, the Poles suffered extensively under the Nazis. Word of the abominations in occupied Poland reached the Allies during the war. However, the extent of the tragedy would only come to light as Allied forces began liberating Nazi-occupied territory.

Today, these crimes against humanity are collectively known as the Holocaust. The Nazis' murder of Jews is called the *Shoah* which means "catastrophe" or "disaster". Approximately six million Jews were murdered. Even today, it is unknown how many people overall fell victim to the genocide. The numbers range anywhere from 9 to 17 million, depending on the criteria used.

12.2.10 Analyze how ideological conflict shaped international relations after the Second World War

HOW IDEOLOGICAL CONFLICT SHAPED INTERNATIONAL RELATIONS

THE COLD WAR

With the end of the Second World War, two nations emerged as superpowers: the United States and the Soviet Union. Relations between these two superpowers were poor. The United States was a liberal, democratic, and capitalist nation; the Soviet Union was a collectivist, totalitarian, and Communist nation. However, the two nations never openly warred with one another. With the advent of nuclear weaponry, open warfare would have resulted in the annihilation of both nations and possibly the rest of the planet. Instead, the superpowers competed to spread and protect their respective ideologies. This period, which lasted from the end of the Second World War until the collapse of the Soviet Union in 1991, is known as the Cold War.

Spheres of Influence

Each superpower adopted a sphere of influence—an area of the world in which one superpower was dominant. These areas often became battlegrounds, where the superpowers competed to expand their own influence or limit that of the other. Vietnam, Korea, Cambodia, Cuba, Iran, Afghanistan, and many other countries fought what were, in effect, proxy battles for the superpowers.

To solidify their spheres of influence, each superpower founded international alliances based on mutual protection, which meant that an attack on one ally would be construed as an attack on all those in the alliance. The United States led NATO (the North Atlantic Treaty Organization), which was founded in Washington, D.C. in 1949. Prominent members included Canada, the United Kingdom, France, which withdrew in 1966, West Germany, Italy, Norway, and several other European nations. None of the member nations invoked the mutual defence clause until 2001, following the terrorist attacks on the United States on September 11.

The Soviet Union created an organization of its own in response to the inclusion of West Germany in NATO. In 1955, the Communist states of Eastern and Central Europe signed the Treaty of Friendship, Cooperation, and Mutual Assistance, more commonly known as the Warsaw Pact. In theory, the Warsaw Pact promised mutual protection and respect for each member's sovereignty. In practice, the Soviet Union used the Warsaw Pact to create a buffer zone between itself and Western Europe, and they often interfered in the affairs of member nations. For example, they invaded Hungary in 1956 and Czechoslovakia in 1968 in order to maintain their buffer zone. Winston Churchill famously referred to this buffer zone as the Iron Curtain.

Non-Alignment

Many nations chose not to align themselves with one superpower or the othe. Nations from every political spectrum chose to stay neutral in the ideological conflict between the superpowers. France withdrew from NATO in 1966, and chose to pursue its own policies. Likewise, Yugoslavia, under the control of Communist leader Josip Broz Tito, charted its own course. Yugoslavia was a founding member of the Non-Aligned Movement, along with Egypt, India, Indonesia, and Ghana.

Containment and Deterrence

American foreign policy during the Cold War was one of containment. If a nation looked vulnerable to a communist takeover, then the United States would intervene. This intervention was generally financial (backing anti-communist elements or regimes), but the United States would occasionally employ direct military intervention. This practice was controversial, since the anti-communist regimes were often brutal totalitarian governments.

The superpowers had to be careful of the extent to which they interfered with one another's spheres of influence. The primary deterrent was the enormous nuclear arsenal each superpower possessed. Many argued (and still argue) that the concept of—mutual assured destruction—(MAD) resulted in relative peace. After all, neither superpower could attack the other without causing its own destruction. However, certain events brought the world to the brink of nuclear war.

The Cuban Missile Crisis

During the Cold War, most Communist nations were in Europe and Asia, with the exception of Cuba. This was deeply troubling to the United States, since Cuba is only miles from its southern coast. Attempts by the United States to intervene in Cuba's affairs failed, including a disastrous CIA-backed invasion (the Bay of Pigs invasion) in 1961. Fearing further attacks, Cuban leader Fidel Castro openly aligned himself with the Soviet Union. In October 1962, American spy planes captured images of missile bases being built in Cuba.

American President John F. Kennedy ordered a blockade of Cuba and threatened the Soviet Union with massive retaliation should any missiles be launched from the Cuban bases. In response, Soviet Premier Nikita Khrushchev declared the blockade illegal and promised retaliation should the Americans interfere with Soviet ships. This brinkmanship demonstrated the unwillingness of both superpowers to back down, and it escalated the crisis. Soon, however, the superpowers reached a consensus: the Cuban missile bases would be abandoned in exchange for the Americans decommissioning their missile bases in Turkey. Also, the Americans agreed to desist in their attempts to overthrow Castro or otherwise interfere in Cuban sovereignty.

Détente

By the early 1970s, both superpowers were growing weary of the constant tension, the arms race, and the petty conflicts. The nuclear arms race was incredibly expensive, and it heavily burdened the superpowers' economies. There was increasing civil and political unrest in the United States, citizens were protesting against nuclear proliferation and the unpopular Vietnam War. The Soviet Union had its own problems when a political split with Communist China prompted fears of a Sino-American alliance. Thus, it was in the best interest of both nations to ease tensions. This is known as détente (French for "easing").

The détente period is marked by a series of treaties between the superpowers. These treaties were drafted to limit the nuclear arsenals of the superpowers and to prevent the development of nuclear weapons in other countries. The most important treaties are as follows:

• Nuclear Non-Proliferation Treaty - (NPT), 1968 - Under its terms, only the United States, Soviet Union, United Kingdom, China, and France were permitted to possess, acquire, manufacture, or otherwise obtain nuclear weapons.

• The first Strategic Arms Limitation Treaty - (SALT I), 1972 -Under its terms, the superpowers agreed not to increase the number of strategic ballistic missile launchers beyond existing levels.

• Anti-Ballistic Missile Treaty - (ABM Treaty), 1972 - Under its terms, the superpowers agreed not to build up defences against ballistic missiles, which could have upset the balance of power and caused another expensive arms race.

• The second Strategic Arms Limitation Treaty- (SALT II), 1979 . The treaty was never actually ratified by the United States, but both superpowers abided by its terms, which imposed further limits and reductions on strategic ballistic missile launchers

The period of détente ended with the Soviet invasion of Afghanistan in 1979, and tensions once again began to rise.

The End of the Cold War

In the 1980s, Soviet General Secretary Mikhail Gorbachev introduced a series of reforms: perestroika (restructuring), reform to the Soviet economy, and glasnost (openness) to reform the Soviet political structure to make it more transparent and free. These reforms went far beyond Gorbachev's intentions. They resulted in the collapse of the Soviet Union. Liberation movements swept through Communist countries. In East Germany and Czechoslovakia, mass popular uprisings toppled their Communist governments in 1989. In the same year, Hungary and Poland organized open, fair elections, and a violent overthrow of the government took place in Romania. Soon, nations that were part of the Soviet Union began to declare their independence, and on December 30, 1991, the Soviet Union was officially dissolved.

12.2.12   Analyze the extent to which modern liberalism is challenged by alternative thought

CONTEMPORARY CHALLENGES TO LIBERAL THOUGHT

ENVIRONMENTALISM

In recent decades, people have become increasingly aware and concerned about the impact human activity has on the environment. There is mounting evidence that pollutants are affecting the global climate. Therefore, the ideology of environmentalism (protection of the environment) has become ever more popular and powerful.

However, environmentalism runs counter to liberalism in many ways. It seeks to place restrictions on the way people use or consume their own property. It promotes government interference in the economy to protect the environment from abuse. In many ways, it is a collectivist ideology, since it places limits on personal freedoms in order to achieve a common goal. This is not necessarily a bad thing; the preservation of the environment is a laudable goal. However, environmentalism comes with economic and social costs that liberal societies have been reluctant to pay.

NEOCONSERVATISM

Neoconservatism is a reaction to modern liberalism. Its adherents believe that modern liberalism, in many ways, fails to address contemporary political, social, and economic realities. Neoconservatism's major influence is on foreign policy; it favours a proactive approach. Thus, neoconservatism was popular during the Cold War, and neoconservative politicians fully supported American interference in foreign nations in order to support anti-communist groups or regimes. Neoconservatism regained popularity after the terrorist attacks of September 11, 2001; the United States government has toppled two regimes (in Afghanistan and Iraq) that it deemed hostile or dangerous to the United States.

Economically, many neoconservatives are comfortable with the modern welfare state, although they are inclined to oppose government interference in the economy. Some neoconservative economists, such as Milton Friedman, advocate a return to classical liberal economics: minimum taxation, few (if any) social programs, and complete deregulation of industries and services. Because neoconservatives favour proactive foreign policy, they tend to favour increased military spending.

PRACTICE QUESTIONS—RELATED ISSUE 2

1. Which of the following ideas was the Baron de Montesquieu's **most important** contribution to liberal-democratic ideology?
   A. Universal suffrage
   B. Freedom of speech
   C. Separation of powers
   D. Laissez-faire economics

2. Which of the following purposes **most clearly** defines what John Locke saw as the primary role of the state?
   A. To ensure the security of the populace
   B. To distribute goods fairly among citizens
   C. To allow the accumulation of private property
   D. To make important decisions on behalf of citizens

3. Which of the following situations did **not** occur as a result of mercantilism?
   A. Increased organization of industrial workers
   B. Frequent conflict between European nations
   C. Constant government interference in the economy
   D. The rise of huge government-sponsored monopolies

4. Adam Smith felt that nations could become wealthy **most effectively** by
   A. nationalizing key industries
   B. imposing high taxes on trade
   C. protecting all domestic businesses
   D. allowing free trade with other countries

5. According to Adam Smith, what is the **primary** source of a commodity's value?
   A. The rarity of the commodity
   B. The demand for the commodity
   C. The usefulness of the commodity
   D. The labour that produced the commodity

6. Adam Smith's concept of the "invisible hand" refers to the
   A. interaction of supply and demand
   B. ability of the free market to regulate itself
   C. tendency of people to act in their own interests
   D. government practice of minimal economic interference

7. Which of the following phrases **best** describes the meaning of the term *laissez-faire*?
   A. Free trade
   B. Do the least
   C. Self-interest
   D. Leave it alone

8. Which of the following political ideas did **not** affect the original United States Constitution?
   A. Baron de Montesquieu's *Spirit of the Laws*
   B. John Locke's *Two Treatises of Government*
   C. The laws of the Haudenosaunee Confederacy
   D. The constitution of the French revolutionaries

9. Which of the following abuses was **not** typical of early industrial workplaces?
   A. Use of child labour
   B. Extremely low wages
   C. Refusal to hire women
   D. Unsafe working conditions

10. Which of the following major political changes occurred in Great Britain as a result of the labour movement?
    A. The illegalization of unions
    B. The extension of the franchise
    C. The overthrow of the monarchy
    D. The election of a socialist government

11. Socialism is **most closely** related to which of the following ideologies?
    A. Fascism
    B. Capitalism
    C. Communism
    D. Totalitarianism

12. Which of the following statements is **not** a part of communist doctrine?

A. Private property should be abolished entirely.

B. The economy should be in the hands of the government.

C. Private property is the source of the division between the classes.

D. Capitalism should be gradually phased out to end the class struggle.

13. What is the title of John Stuart Mill's foundational work on liberalism?

A. *On Liberty*

B. *Rights of Man*

C. *Rerum Novarum*

D. *The Wealth of Nations*

14. According to John Stuart Mill, the oppression of women and minorities results from a

A. perceived imbalance

B. form of social tyranny

C. tyranny of the majority

D. struggle between the classes

15. Keynesian economics is also known as

A. monetarist economics

B. supply-side economics

C. demand-side economics

D. trickle-down economics

16. Who was the **first** leader of the Soviet Union?

A. Joseph Stalin

B. Leon Trotsky

C. Yuri Andropov

D. Vladimir Lenin

17. What was the **main** purpose of Lenin's New Economic Policy?

A. To revitalize the economy following war communism

B. To supply the Soviet armed forces with necessary goods

C. To move from small-scale collectives to a command economy

D. To eliminate the last vestiges of capitalism in the Soviet Union

18. Under Stalin, opposition was directly eliminated through imprisonment, deportation to labour camps, show trials, and executions. These methods are collectively known as

A. purges

B. cleansings

C. liquidations

D. purifications

19. The Nazi Party's paramilitary wing, which intimidated and attacked opposition, was called the

A. *Schutzstaffel*

B. *Einsatzgruppen*

C. *Sturmabteilung*

D. *Geheime Staatspolizei*

20. Which of the following phrases describes the **main** purpose of *Aktion T4*?

A. To establish extermination camps in occupied areas

B. To euthanize people with mental or physical handicaps

C. To bypass France's defences by attacking through Belgium

D. To target Jewish homes, businesses, and places of worship for vandalism

21. How did the Allies respond when they first learned of Nazi atrocities in occupied areas?

A. They dismissed the reports and took no action.

B. They provided support to Jewish resistance groups.

C. They launched Operation Sea Lion to rescue camp inmates.

D. They destroyed the city of Dresden in a massive bombing campaign.

22. What was the name of the Communist nations' mutual protection pact?

A. The Kiev Pact

B. The Berlin Pact

C. The Warsaw Pact

D. The Moscow Pact

23. The United States reacted to the discovery of missile bases in Cuba in 1962 by

A. invading Cuba

B. blockading Cuba

C. threatening to attack Cuba

D. backing an invasion of Cuba

24. The superpowers signed the Anti-Ballistic Missile Treaty **mainly** because they wanted to

   A. avoid nuclear proliferation

   B. avoid another expensive arms race

   C. limit stockpiles of ballistic missiles

   D. protect themselves from nuclear attack

25. If a government had a budget surplus, a neoconservative citizen would **most likely** favour applying the extra money to

   A. health-care programs

   B. military infrastructure

   C. tax cuts for businesses

   D. environmental protection

Use the following information to answer the next question.

> • Wealth distributed equally among workers
> • Means of production collectively owned
> • Resources controlled by the public
> • Cooperation over competition

26. The given ideas best describe the economic system of which political ideology?

   A. Socialism

   B. Liberalism

   C. Conservatism

   D. Totalitarianism

Use the following information to answer the next question.

> I believe the economy is unstable and that the government should help regulate the economy by reducing taxes and spending more money on infrastructure during times of recession.

27. The given statement would most likely have been made by

   A. Karl Marx

   B. Adam Smith

   C. John Steward Mill

   D. John Maynard Keynes

28. Labour standards and unions would not be tolerated by which type of government?

    A. Liberal

    B. Socialist

    C. Totalitarian

    D. Conservative

29. Which of the following regulation would not be part of a welfare state?

    A. Maternity leave

    B. Medical insurance

    C. Minimum-wage laws

    D. Fifteen - hour work days

Use the following information to answer the next question.

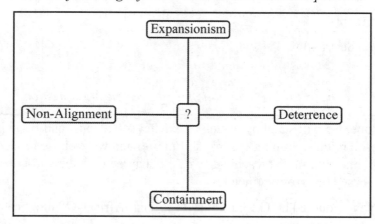

30. Each of the given foreign-policy strategies was part of world political affairs during which time period?

    A. The Cold War

    B. The Vietnam War

    C. The First World War

    D. The Second World War

Use the following information to answer the next question.

Two opposing sides amass weapons of mass destruction, through which a direct conflict would result in the annihilation of both sides.

31. The given statement is an example of which method of war?
    A. Deterrence
    B. Containment
    C. Expansionism
    D. Non-alignment

32. A period of reduced tension during a conflict is known as
    A. détente
    B. dissuasion
    C. liberation movements
    D. mutually assured destruction

Use the following information to answer the next question.

If we have to stand alone, we will stand by ourselves, whatever happens (and India has stood alone without any aid against a mighty Empire, the British Empire) and we propose to face all consequences ...We do not agree with the communist teachings, we do not agree with the anti-communist teachings, because they are both based on wrong principles.

—Jawaharlal Nehru, quoted by G.M. Kahin, The Asian-African Conference (New York: Cornell University Press, 1956), pp. 64–72

33. The given quotation by India's former prime minister Jawaharlal Nehru is an example of
    A. deterrence
    B. containment
    C. expansionism
    D. non-alignment

Use the following information to answer the next question.

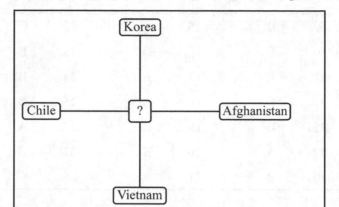

34. From the 1950's through the 1980's, in connection with the Cold War, the given countries experienced

A. détente

B. dissuasion

C. liberation movements

D. mutually assured destruction

ANSWERS AND SOLUTIONS—PRACTICE QUESTIONS

1.	C	8.	D	15.	C	22.	C	29.	D
2.	C	9.	C	16.	D	23.	B	30.	A
3.	A	10.	B	17.	A	24.	B	31.	A
4.	D	11.	C	18.	A	25.	B	32.	A
5.	D	12.	D	19.	C	26.	A	33.	D
6.	C	13.	A	20.	B	27.	D	34.	C
7.	D	14.	B	21.	A	28.	C		

1. C

Montesquieu's idea of the separation of powers (into executive, legislative, and judicial branches) is a cornerstone of modern liberal democracy.

The idea of universal suffrage was adopted gradually and was not one of Montesquieu's concepts. Various interpretations of free speech have appeared throughout human history; the liberal-democratic ideal was developed primarily by John Stuart Mill. Laissez-faire economics was Adam Smith's idea.

2. C

Locke saw the ownership of property as the key to individual sovereignty (power over oneself). Therefore, in his view, the most important role of the state is to allow citizens to accumulate and protect property.

3. A

Industrial workers did not begin to organize until after the Industrial Revolution.

By the time of the Industrial Revolution, the mercantile system had largely been replaced by free market economics.

4. D

Adam Smith felt that governments should avoid interfering in the economy. Therefore, he would oppose government control of industries, high trade taxes, and protection of local businesses. According to Smith, free trade is the way to national prosperity.

5. D

Adam Smith believed that the effort required to obtain, produce, transport, manufacture, or create a commodity is the source of its value.

For example, a cotton dress is worth more than the cloth needed to make it; and the cloth is more valuable than the raw cotton with which it is made. The difference between the three is the labour involved in obtaining or creating them.

6. C

The "invisible hand" is Adam Smith's description of how people working for their own interests can unintentionally benefit society as a whole.

7. D

The term *laissez-faire* is a French and although it literally translates to "leave to do", the phrase "leave it alone" captures the sense of the term better.

It describes a state of affairs in which the government does not interfere in the economy. In other words, the government leaves it alone.

8. D

The French Revolution did not take place until after the American Constitution was drafted.

The constitution was heavily influenced by the work of Locke and Montesquieu, as well as the example of the Haudenosaunee Confederacy.

9. C

Factories did not refuse to hire women; they simply paid them lower wages than men. Even men's wages were extremely low, so their wives and children often had to work factory jobs to help the family survive.

The working conditions were unsafe. Accidents and work-related illnesses such as coal-dust inhalation were common.

10. B

Pressure from the labour movement caused the government to extend the franchise (right to vote) to the working classes by the end of the nineteenth century.

11. C

Communism is, in essence, an extreme form of socialism.

12. D

Communists believe the working class should violently seize the means of production from the wealthy class. Mainstream socialists believe in a gradual end to class differences.

13. A

Mill's *On Liberty* is the foundation of liberal political thought.

Rights of Man was written by Thomas Paine, an important figure in the American and French revolutions. *Rerum Novarum* is a papal encyclical on the nature of capital and labour. *The Wealth of Nations* by Adam Smith is the foundation of classical liberal economic thought.

14. B

Mill felt that women and minorities were held back by people's preconceived notions of their capabilities. These groups were under considerable social pressure to adhere to the roles that mainstream society assigned to them which is a form of social tyranny.

15. C

Because Keynesian economics focuses on the regulation of consumer demand, it is known as demand-side economics.

16. D

Vladimir Ilyich Ulyanov, better known as Lenin, officially became leader of the Soviet Union in November, 1918.

After Lenin's death, Trotsky and Stalin vied for the leadership, with Stalin emerging as the victor. Andropov's short reign did not begin until 1982.

17. A

War communism succeeded in keeping the Red Army supplied, but virtually ruined the Soviet economy. Therefore, Lenin was forced to reintroduce a limited amount of capitalism in order to revitalize the economy. This plan was the New Economic Policy.

During Stalin's reign, most of those who had become wealthy from the New Economic Policy (derogatorily known as "NEPmen") were deemed class traitors and purged.

18. A

The Stalinist purges, especially the Great Purge of 1936 to 1938, eliminated Stalin's political rivals and those who objected to his policies.

19. C

The *Sturmabteilung* (SA, or "assault detachment") was a paramilitary organization used to intimidate political opposition, harass Jews, and perform other violent actions. Once Hitler grew powerful enough, he had the SA purged as a threat to his authority.

The dreaded *Geheime Staatspolizei* (*Gestapo* or "secret state police") was a secret police force that operated outside the law. The *Schutzstaffel* ("protection squad") was an elite and fanatically loyal paramilitary force that was responsible for the bulk of the Nazi atrocities. The *Einsatzgruppen* ("special task forces") eliminated racial and political enemies in Nazi-occupied territory.

20. B

***Aktion T4* was intended to ensure the racial purity of the German people by eliminating those with mental or physical disabilities. This was done under the pretence of euthanasia, or mercy killing.**

The establishment of the extermination camps was called the Final Solution (*Endlösung*). The Nazi attack against France was called blitzkrieg ("lightning war"). The attacks on Jewish homes, businesses, and places of worship are generally known as pogroms. The worst pogrom was Kristallnacht (the Night of Broken Glass), which occurred November 9, 1938.

21. A

Unfortunately, the Allies (along with most people and groups outside the occupied areas) did not believe the reports. They were seen as impossible, as gross exaggerations, or as propaganda from the exiled Polish government. Therefore, the Allies did not support the Jewish or Polish resistance.

Operation Sea Lion was the Nazi plan to invade England, not a rescue plan. The controversial bombing of Dresden was conducted to demoralize the Germans and destroy important factories.

22. C

The Warsaw Pact was signed in 1955; its official name is the Treaty of Friendship, Cooperation, and Mutual Assistance.

23. B

United States President John F. Kennedy ordered a naval blockade of Cuba.

The Americans did not invade or threaten to attack Cuba. They had backed an invasion there by Cuban exiles in 1961. That invasion was a disaster and merely encouraged Cuban leader Fidel Castro to forge closer ties with the Soviet Union.

24. B

Anti-ballistic missiles, or ABMs, are designed to destroy nuclear missiles before they can reach their targets. In order to maintain the balance of power, both superpowers would have had to spend billions of dollars on ABM development, as well as on technology to defeat ABMs. Neither nation wanted to engage in another expensive arms race, so they agreed not to develop or deploy ABMs.

25. B

Because neoconservatives favour a strong military as the best means of effecting international change, a neoconservative would most likely favour spending on military infrastructure.

26. A

Socialism is the ideology that includes the belief that the means of production should be collectively owned and wealth should be distributed among the workers.

Conservatism believes in a more hands-off approach to the economy, allowing a free market to regulate itself. A liberal economic system is usually a combination of socialist and conservative economic ideas, similar to the economic system in Canada. A totalitarian approach to the economy usually only benefits the state and the people most closely connected to the state.

27. D

John Maynard Keynes proposed a system of government regulation designed to even out the boom-bust cycle that is often seen in a free market economy. Keynes also believed that during times of inflation, the government should spend less money and increase taxes to help keep inflation in check.

28. C

A totalitarian government seeks to regulate almost every part of its citizens' lives, from the economy to the media. This type of government would not tolerate labour unions.

29. D

A 15-hour work day would not be part of the regulations of a welfare state.

Minimum-wage laws, medical insurance, maternity leave, and standard work hours would all be part of government regulations put in place to protect employees.

30. A

During the Cold War, which took place from the end of the Second World War to the early 1990s, the United States and the Soviet Union each practised these foreign policies.

31. A

Deterrence **is a method of war that is used during a cold war not a hot war. It involves the fortification of one's miliatry and weaponry to the point of mutually assured destruction, whereby a war would ensure the destruction of both sides (and possibly the rest of the world). Thus, both countries would be deterred from entering into conflict.**

Both the Soviet Union and the United States used expansionism to enlarge their territorial and ideological influence beyond their own borders. Both countries also used containment to try to stop the expansion and influence of the other country. Non-alignment is the term used to describe the policy of countries that refused to take sides during the Cold War, choosing to remain neutral instead.

32. A

Détente **is a French word that means "relaxing" or "easing". It is a period of reduced tension between nations that have been hostile, but not involved in a hot war.**

It is generally used to describe the easing of tensions between the United States and the Soviet Union from the mid-1960's to 1979, when the Soviet Union invaded Afghanistan.

33. D

Non-alignment is the term used to describe the policy of many countries that refused to take sides during the Cold War, choosing to remain netrual instead . The given quote by India's prime minster explains why his country chose to remain neutral and stand on its own.

34. C

Liberation movements are when a group within a country, or the whole nation, rebels against the country that has colonized it or otherwise oppressed it. These liberation movements are sometimes funded and supported by another superpower that opposes the colonizing country.

UNIT TEST—RELATED ISSUE 2

1. Which of the following statements describes how Thomas Hobbes believed humans would act in the absence of the state?

   A. They would cooperate for mutual benefit.

   B. They would freely steal from and kill one another.

   C. They would be dominated by the strongest person.

   D. They would struggle amongst themselves for resources.

2. Jean-Jacques Rousseau believed the ideal government would be

   A. a direct democracy

   B. an absolute monarchy

   C. a constitutional monarchy

   D. a representative democracy

3. What is the name of Adam Smith's foundational work on liberal economics?

   A. *The Wealth of Nations*

   B. *Discourse on Inequality*

   C. *Principles of Economics*

   D. *The Philosophy of Poverty*

4. Under mercantilism, nations **mainly** measured their wealth by the amount of

   A. land they held

   B. trade they conducted

   C. goods they generated

   D. bullion they possessed

5. Adam Smith believed that citizens could help the economy the **most** by

   A. purchasing more goods

   B. purchasing fewer goods

   C. acting in their own interests

   D. charging less for goods and services

Use the following information to answer the next question.

Four different people in business were asked for their opinions on international trade.

Speaker I

In international trade, the best deal is one in which both sides benefit. It's perfectly possible for both sides of a trade to come away happy; you get what you need, and they get what they need. I don't want to hurt my trading partners because I want to keep doing business with them.

Speaker II

Trade is a competition, and in any competition, there are winners and losers. I'm in business to make money, not to prop up foreign companies. If I can take advantage of them, I will. It may sound harsh, but that's the way the game is played.

Speaker III

International trade is important, but you have to be careful. It's important to have a strong domestic economy, and international trade can undercut that. If the government doesn't protect domestic trade, businesses can go under, and that means lost jobs and lost tax revenue.

Speaker IV

International trade is, at best, a necessary evil. A nation isn't truly strong unless it is self-sufficient. Why would you want to send your capital to a foreign country? Who wants to have to rely on another nation for necessary goods? International trade is only good for selling off surplus; anything more just weakens the country.

6. Which speaker would Adam Smith **most likely** agree with?

   A. Speaker I

   B. Speaker II

   C. Speaker III

   D. Speaker IV

7. Edmund Burke believed strongly in the value of

   A. social contract theory

   B. the authority of the monarch

   C. the will and desire of the citizenry

   D. traditional practices and institutions

8. Which of the following social changes occurred **mainly** as a result of the Industrial Revolution?

   A. The increase in urban populations

   B. The abandonment of mercantilism

   C. The extension of voting rights to workers

   D. The increase in hardships for the working poor

9. According to socialist economic theory, the means of production should be owned by
    A. collectives
    B. corporations
    C. governments
    D. entrepreneurs

10. What is the name of the German philosopher who, along with Karl Marx, largely developed communism?
    A. Friedrich Lang
    B. Friedrich Hayek
    C. Friedrich Engels
    D. Friedrich Nietzsche

11. According to John Stuart Mill, the two freedoms essential to liberal society are
    A. freedom of speech and freedom of the press
    B. freedom of the press and freedom of religion
    C. freedom of religion and freedom of association
    D. freedom of association and freedom to bear arms

12. The foundation of the American welfare state was laid out in
    A. George Marshall's Marshall Plan
    B. Franklin D. Roosevelt's New Deal
    C. John F. Kennedy's Civil Rights Act
    D. Theodore Roosevelt's progressivism

13. Which of the following actions describes the **main** purpose of Stalin's five-year plans?
    A. To hold periodic one-party elections in the soviets
    B. To build up the Soviet Union's nuclear arms stockpile
    C. To regularly identify and eliminate potential dissidents
    D. To provide quotas for industrial and agricultural production

14. The *Holodomor* of 1932 to 1933 was a great famine in one of the most agriculturally rich areas in the Eurasian continent, resulting in at least 6 million deaths. In which of the following countries did this famine occur?
    A. Latvia
    B. Russia
    C. Estonia
    D. Ukraine

15. Which of the following situations did **not** contribute to the failure of liberalism in Germany between the World Wars?

    A. The increasing popularity of the Nazi party

    B. The humiliation caused by the Treaty of Versailles

    C. The popularity of the pre-war socialist government

    D. The weakness and instability of the Weimar government

16. By which of the following methods did the Nazis gain control of Germany?

    A. By assaulting or murdering their political opponents

    B. By violently overthrowing the weak Weimar government

    C. By receiving aid from Mussolini's fascist government in Italy

    D. By winning a majority in the German Parliament, the Reichstag

17. For which of the following reasons were the nations of Europe **most likely** willing to concede to Hitler's demands?

    A. They feared Germany's military strength.

    B. They were war-weary after the First World War.

    C. They believed that Hitler's demands were justified.

    D. They wanted to help Germany recover from its economic collapse.

18. Which of the following nations left NATO in 1966?

    A. France

    B. Poland

    C. West Germany

    D. United Kingdom

19. Which of the following statements regarding the advantage of the Warsaw Pact to the Soviet Union is **true**?

    A. The Soviet Union gained a buffer zone between itself and western Europe.

    B. The Warsaw Pact intimidated western European nations into staying neutral.

    C. The Warsaw Pact extended the Soviet sphere of influence into Central Europe.

    D. The Soviet Union could legally intervene in the affairs of Warsaw Pact nations..

20. Which of the following nations was **not** a member of the Warsaw Pact?

    A. Albania

    B. Bulgaria

    C. Yugoslavia

    D. Czechoslovakia

21. Which of the following situations brought the superpowers to the brink of open warfare?
    A. The Sino-Soviet Split
    B. The Cuban Missile Crisis
    C. The Prague Spring Reforms
    D. The Gulf of Tonkin Incident

22. Which of the following factors did **not** contribute to détente (the easing of tensions between the United States and the Soviet Union)?
    A. Development of anti-ballistic missile technology
    B. The Sino-Soviet Split between China and the Soviet Union
    C. Popular unrest over nuclear proliferation and constant conflict
    D. The financial burden of building and maintaining large nuclear arsenals

23. Which of the following treaties limited the possession of nuclear weapons to the United States, the Soviet Union, the United Kingdom, China, and France?
    A. NPT
    B. ABMT
    C. SALT I
    D. SALT II

24. Which of the following events ended the détente period?
    A. The American invasion of Cuba
    B. The collapse of the Soviet Union
    C. The Soviet invasion of Afghanistan
    D. The advent of glasnost and perestroika

Use the following information to answer the next question.

Four American citizens were asked the question "When is the use of military force justified?"

Speaker I

The military exists to serve the nation. If there's something the nation is lacking, then using military force to get it is always an option, especially if that resource is essential to the country. It sounds cruel, but that's the way the world is sometimes.

Speaker II

The United States is facing its greatest threat since the fall of the Soviet Union. We can't afford to sit back. Any time a nation threatens peace, freedom, or human rights, we should use military force to quell it. We have the power to bring democracy and liberty to the world; why not do so?

Speaker III

We are a strong nation, but we shouldn't act like we're the world's police force. If military force is needed, that should be decided by the global community—in other words, by the United Nations. Only with UN approval is military force justified.

Speaker IV

Military force should only be used as a last resort. It is rarely as effective as diplomacy or economic measures. By talking and trading with other nations, we can come to a common understanding. The military should only be used for defence and for peacekeeping.

25. Which of the speakers is **mostly likely** a neoconservative?

   A. Speaker I

   B. Speaker II

   C. Speaker III

   D. Speaker IV

Use the following information to answer the next question.

- Workers own the means of production
- The proletariat against the bourgeoisie
- The Communist Manifesto
- The workers' revolution

26. The given points best describe the ideas of

   A. Karl Marx

   B. Adam Smith

   C. Robert Owen

   D. Edmund Burke

Use the following information to answer the next question.

27. The given advertisement is an example of the ideas involved in

A. communism

B. conservatism

C. welfare capitalism

D. laissez-faire economics

ANSWERS AND SOLUTIONS—UNIT TEST

1.	D	7.	D	13.	D	19.	A	25.	B
2.	A	8.	A	14.	D	20.	C	26.	A
3.	A	9.	A	15.	C	21.	B	27.	C
4.	D	10.	C	16.	D	22.	A		
5.	C	11.	A	17.	B	23.	A		
6.	A	12.	B	18.	A	24.	C		

1. D

Hobbes envisioned the natural state of humans as an "everyone for themselves" scenario, in which people would ensure their own survival and happiness at the expense of others. Only the authority of an absolute ruler (Hobbes' *Leviathan*) could protect humans from one another.

Hobbes did not believe humans were evil; they might argue and fight, but they would not steal or murder for the fun of it.

2. A

Rousseau believed that every citizen should vote directly on legislation (i.e., direct democracy). He felt this would allow people to return to their natural state of cooperation and community.

3. A

Adam Smith wrote *An Inquiry into the Nature and Causes of the Wealth of Nations*, which is generally known as *The Wealth of Nations*.

Discourse on Inequality was written by French Enlightenment philosopher Jean-Jacques Rousseau. *Principles of Economics* is a textbook written by English political economist Alfred Marshall. French anarchist philosopher Pierre-Joseph Proudhon wrote *The Philosophy of Poverty*.

4. D

The mercantile nations of Europe measured their wealth in terms of bullion (bulk forms of precious metals like gold and silver).

Land was a measure of wealth for individuals, not nations. During the mercantile period, governments freely interfered with the economy. The idea was to rely as little as possible on foreign trade rather than grow wealthy through trade. By producing their own goods, nations could hoard bullion instead of having to use it to purchase goods from other nations.

5. C

When citizens act in their own interests, they unintentionally benefit the economy. Smith refers to this as the "invisible hand."

The number of goods they purchase, or the amount they pay for goods, will depend on the regulation of the free market by the "invisible hand." Note that Smith does not actually advocate self-interest—he simply believes that the tendency of people to act in their own interests is economically beneficial.

6. A

Speaker I recognizes that two businesses, each acting in their own interests, can mutually benefit from trade. This concept is an important part of Adam Smith's economic viewpoint.

Speakers II, III, and IV all display aspects of mercantile ideology, which is trade cannot be mutually beneficial, that the government should protect domestic trade, and that international trade weakens nations.

7. D

Burke essentially founded modern conservatism, and had a very practical view of politics and society. He believed that traditions were absolutely necessary for society to function properly. In effect, they were guidelines for correct behaviour, morality, and civility.

Burke scorned social contract theory and was skeptical of the ability of both citizens and rulers to choose the correct course for society. For example, he was horrified by the French Revolution (the will of the people), which he correctly predicted would end in chaos and mob rule. On the other hand, he supported the American Revolution. He believed England was abusing its power over the colonists (the authority of the monarch).

8. A

The Industrial Revolution sparked a massive influx of labour from rural areas into the cities.

Mercantilism had been dismantled by the time of the Industrial Revolution. Workers did not receive voting rights until well into the industrial era, and they received them as a result of the labour movement, not the Industrial Revolution. Finally, although conditions for the working poor were terrible during the industrial period, they were not much different from those of the Middle Ages and the early modern era.

9. A

Socialist economic theory states that the means of production should be owned by workers' collectives.

10. C

Friedrich Engels co-wrote *The Communist Manifesto* with Karl Marx.

Friedrich Lang was a German pilot in the Second World War. Friedrich Hayek was an Austrian economic philosopher and staunch opponent of socialism. Friedrich Nietzsche was a German existential philosopher.

11. A

According to Mill, a healthy society depends on the open and free exchange of ideas. Therefore, freedom of speech and freedom of the press are essential.

12. B

The New Deal provided a number of economic and social welfare initiatives: public works projects, stock-market regulation, bank deposit insurance, social security, and labour standards. These are the foundation of the modern welfare state.

The Marshall Plan was a massive economic recovery program aimed at restoring Europe after the Second World War and checking the spread of communism. The Civil Rights Act was an important step toward ending racial discrimination in America. Theodore Roosevelt's progressivism helped protect industrial workers from exploitation, but the changes were nowhere near as radical as those in the New Deal.

13. D

The Soviet Union was decades behind most Western nations in terms of industrial and agricultural production. The five-year plans were designed to accelerate the Soviet Union's growth by providing strict production quotas.

In essence, all the resources of the Soviet Union were applied to addressing the imbalances. In one sense, this was of great benefit to the Soviet Union. Its new industrial power allowed it to fend off the Nazi invasion and emerge from the Second World War as a superpower. However, the five-year plans severely disrupted citizens' lives and, in extreme cases, led to widespread starvation and displacement.

14. **D**

The great famine in Ukraine was caused by the policies of Stalin in the Soviet Union.

Some maintain that the famine was accidental while others argue that it was a deliberate act of genocide. The first monument to commemorate the Holodomor was erected in Edmonton in 1983, largely because Ukrainians were not yet free to do so in their own country.

15. **C**

Before the First World War, Germany was ruled by a popular monarch, Kaiser Wilhelm II, not a socialist government. Many Germans were angry that the kaiser had been forced to abdicate as part of the conditions of peace.

16. **D**

Although the Nazis employed strong-arm tactics to intimidate their political rivals, they actually gained control of Germany through democratic means: by winning enough seats in the *Reichstag* to form the government. Once Hitler was appointed chancellor, he used his position to dismantle the republic and form a totalitarian government.

17. **B**

When Hitler began abrogating the Treaty of Versailles and annexing territory, the nations of Europe were still trying to recover from the ravages of the First World War. Therefore, they adopted a policy of appeasement (giving in to demands) in the hopes that Hitler would be satisfied.

They did not particularly fear Germany's military might. Some politicians admired Hitler and respected his demands, but the majority simply wanted to avoid another war. Britain wanted Germany to recover, but France was perfectly content with a weak and impoverished Germany.

18. **A**

Although France remained allied with NATO, it withdrew from membership in 1966 to pursue a more independent defence against the threat of communism.

Poland was not a member of NATO in 1966. West Germany and the United Kingdom both remained in NATO.

19. **A**

The Warsaw Pact effectively gave the Soviet Union a buffer zone between itself and the ideologically hostile nations of western Europe, many of whom were members of NATO.

The Warsaw Pact did not give the Soviet Union permission to interfere in the affairs of member nations. In fact, such interference violated the terms of the Warsaw Pact. The Warsaw Pact merely formalized the Soviet sphere of influence in eastern and central Europe; it did not extend it, nor did it serve to intimidate western European nations into neutrality.

20. C

Yugoslavia, under the leadership of Josip Broz Tito, rejected the Warsaw Pact. Tito's relationship with Stalin was tense. Yugoslavia was a founding member of the Non-Aligned Movement.

21. B

The Cuban Missile Crisis, in which American spy planes captured photos of nuclear missile bases being built in Cuba, dramatically escalated tensions between the superpowers.

The Sino-Soviet Split was the ideological clash between Communist China and the Soviet Union. The Prague Spring Reforms led to the Soviet invasion of Czechoslovakia, in violation of the Warsaw Pact. The Gulf of Tonkin Incident was a minor naval battle used as justification for increased American involvement in Southeast Asia (and Vietnam in particular).

22. A

Anti-ballistic missiles are designed to destroy nuclear missiles before they can reach their targets. These actually contributed to increased tensions, as they could upset the balance of power between the superpowers. If a superpower were effectively protected from nuclear attack, it could act with impunity.

23. A

The Nuclear Non-Proliferation Treaty (NPT), was signed in order to prevent nuclear weapons technology from spreading to other nations.

The Anti-Ballistic Missile Treaty (ABMT), forbade the deployment of anti-ballistic missiles. The Strategic Arms Limitation Treaty agreements (SALT) placed limits on the missile launch capabilities of the superpowers.

24. C

The Soviet invasion of Afghanistan in 1979 ended the détente period.

The Americans never actually invaded Cuba, although they backed a force of Cuban exiles in the 1961 Bay of Pigs Invasion. Glasnost and perestroika were reforms launched by Soviet General Secretary Mikhail Gorbachev, and they contributed to the collapse of the Soviet Union in 1991.

25. B

Speaker II supports the use of military force to protect and promote democracy, freedom, and human rights. This is a neoconservative standpoint.

A neoconservative would not be likely to rely on diplomacy (Speaker IV), multilateralism (Speaker III), or support the use of force for material gain (Speaker I).

26. A

Karl Marx wrote *The Communist Manifesto*. He believed the proletariat would rise up against the bourgeoisie and take control of the means of production. He also believed that a workers' revolution would be necessary to bring about change in society.

27. C

Welfare capitalism was a move by industrialists to stop the formation of labour unions. Industrialists used non-monetary rewards to earn the loyalty of their employees. Shorter work days, company housing, and discounts at the company store were all part of welfare capitalism.

NOTES

Related Issue 3

Are the Values of Liberalism Viable?

RELATED ISSUE 3

Table of Correlations		
Specific Expectation	**Practice Questions**	**Unit Test Questions**
By the end of this course, students will:		
12.3 Students will assess the extent to which the principles of liberalism are viable in a contemporary world		
12.3.5 analyze the extent to which the practices of political and economic systems reflect principles of liberalism	1, 2, 3, 4, 5, 7, 8, 15, 18, 19	1, 2, 3, 4, 5, 6, 7, 8, 9, 10
12.3.6 analyze the extent to which liberal democracies reflect illiberal thought and practice	6, 11	11, 13
12.3.7 analyze why the practices of governments may not reflect principles of liberalism	9, 20, 21	12, 14
12.3.8 evaluate the extent to which governments should promote individual and collective rights	10, 12, 16, 17	15, 16, 17, 18, 19, 20
12.3.9 evaluate the extent to which the principles of liberalism are viable in the context of contemporary issues	13, 14, 22, 23	21, 22, 23, 24, 25

RELATED ISSUE 3: TO WHAT EXTENT ARE THE PRINCIPLES OF LIBERALISM VIABLE?

12.3.5   Analyze the extent to which the practices of political and economic systems reflect principles of liberalism

MODERN POLITICAL SYSTEMS

CONSENSUS DECISION-MAKING

Consensus decision-making is a system in which decisions are made through shared discussion, with careful consideration and adoption of minority viewpoints. The members of the group do not need to be elected democratically, although this is frequently the case. Historically, many aboriginal and religious groups have used consensus decision-making in their governance. In present-day Canada, the Northwest Territories and Nunavut employ consensus decision-making instead of the traditional party-based legislative system.

DEMOCRACY

Democracy is the political system most frequently associated with modern liberalism. However, it is possible to have illiberal democracies. For example, in apartheid-era South Africa, the black majority was denied the rights and freedoms provided to the white minority. The government was elected in fair, if unjust, elections; that is, the government did not falsify electoral results to keep itself in power.

In general, liberal democracies do not employ direct democracy; that is, the citizens do not directly participate in approving or rejecting new laws or initiatives. Instead, most liberal democracies are representative—the citizens elect a person to represent them in the government. The only time citizens participate directly in democracy is when the government asks them to vote on a referendum. In Canada, this has occurred three times at the federal level.

A frequent criticism of representative democracy is that it often results in simple majority rule. A majority government (one in which the ruling party has over half the available seats in the legislature or parliament) has a free hand to act as it wishes, provided it does not violate the constitution or the rule of law. In practice, such governments are restrained by the simple fact that if they act irresponsibly, they will not be reelected. The opposition parties ensure that any transgressions are brought to the attention of the public.

AUTHORITARIANISM

An authoritarian government is one in which power is in the hands of an elite group that exercises absolute authority over the state. Authoritarian states vary widely in their composition, treatment of citizens, and the ideals for which they stand. Citizens in authoritarian states have little or no say in politics, especially if they are not affiliated with the ruling power.

Military dictatorships are fairly common in the modern era. These occur when the people in charge of the military use military power to overthrow the legal government, often with the pretext of saving the country from corrupt or inefficient leaders. They tend to be unpopular and brutal, but the citizens have little choice but to endure the ways of the government. During the Cold War era, a superpower might have supported a military dictatorship if it had a similar alignment (to capitalism or communism). Today, military dictatorships lack legitimacy in the international community and are unlikely to be backed by outside sources. As a result, military dictatorships are becoming less common.

In oligarchies, the state is controlled by a few powerful individuals who tend to pass their power on to their children. This is generally done within the context of another political system (including democracy). However, only a few people or families have the political and economic power necessary to hold office. This can be formal, as in the United Arab Emirates, or informal, as in the Russian Federation.

Other forms of authoritarian government exist, including one-party states, absolute monarchies, and theocracies:

- One-party state—Political power rests in the hands of a single party, and no other political parties are allowed to field candidates

- Absolute monarchy—Political power rests in the hands of a hereditary monarch, who passes power to his or her heir (generally a son or daughter, but occasionally another family member)

- Theocracy—Political power rests in the hands of the state's religious leaders, and laws are largely based on interpretations of the religion's holy texts

MODERN ECONOMIC SYSTEMS

TRADITIONAL ECONOMIES

A traditional economy is one in which economic practices have remained largely unchanged over time and are an important part of a community's culture or religion. Such economies rarely incorporate new technologies or practices, and are generally collectivist labour benefits the community as a whole rather than the individual. Traditional economies exist all over the world. Well-known examples include the Amish and the *kibbutzim* of Israel.

Although modern traditional economies are generally small and community-based, they still comprise a large portion of the world's overall economic activity. Approximately 400 million people are employed in traditional economic practices. They can be surprisingly lucrative as well. For example, Iran exports hundreds of millions of dollars worth of handwoven rugs every year.

FREE MARKET ECONOMIES

Although the classical liberal ideal of the free market has fallen out of favour since Adam Smith published his book, *The Wealth of Nations*, it still has its modern proponents. Today, no nation follows a pure free market system, but several smaller communities come close. The best example of this is Hong Kong, a province of China that was once a British colonial possession. Hong Kong is a resource-poor land, so its citizens must trade in order to survive and prosper. Over time, Hong Kong has become immensely wealthy and densely populated.

In modern times, several economists believe that liberal democracies should adopt a free market. Among the most prominent of these was Milton Friedman, who was opposed to any government interference in the economy. He believed that the government's role should be to regulate the money supply, which in turn affects inflation and people's spending habits. Things like health care and education should be privatized, and market forces (Smith's "invisible hand") will make them efficient and cost effective.

COMMAND ECONOMIES

At the other end of the economic spectrum are command economies: systems in which the government completely controls the economy. There is no private property—the government tells citizens what needs to be produced and distributes goods according to where they are needed. The command economy is a cornerstone of communism. In theory, it creates a society without social classes, and all people are economically equal.

In practice, command economies are often inefficient, because they require heavy bureaucratization to coordinate supply with demand. Workers receive no direct compensation for their labour, so the only incentives for them to do their jobs well, are to be inspired by the communist ideal and avoid being punished for poor performance.

MIXED ECONOMIES

In between these extremes lie the mixed economies, which combine elements of the free market with economic welfare programs. The balance between economic freedom and economic equality varies from state to state. Although the concept of the mixed economy is not, in the strictest sense, a liberal concept, modern liberal democracies employ mixed economies. They allow citizens to work in their own interests while shielding them from some of the inequalities that can result under laissez-faire capitalism.

Although mixed economies can be effective, finding the right balance is difficult. Governments must be careful to avoid stifling the economy and accumulating debt by interfering too heavily, but they must also ensure that the needs of the citizens are met. Canada, in recent years, has proved one of the most effective at maintaining the balance. Canada is highly ranked in economic freedom, human development, standard of living, economic stability, and social freedom.

12.3.6   Analyze the extent to which liberal democracies reflect illiberal thought and practice

12.3.7   Analyze why the practices of governments may not reflect principles of liberalism

ILLIBERAL PRACTICES IN LIBERAL DEMOCRACIES

CANADA'S ABORIGINAL PEOPLES

Despite Canada's reputation as a land of economic freedom and social responsibility, the nation has been criticized, both nationally and internationally, for its treatment of Aboriginal Peoples. Canada's history contains many examples of illiberal treatment of First Nations, Inuit, and Métis peoples. Although recent governments have taken measures to address the problems that aboriginal communities face, there is still much work to be done.

Relations between the early European settlers and the Aboriginal Peoples were complicated by differing cultural perspectives. A good example of these differing perspectives is the question of land ownership. To the Aboriginal Peoples, a person does not own land—he or she is part of it, in much the same way as he or she is part of a family or tribe. The land and the people, in essence, belong to one another. The settlers, of course, had different views.

The Europeans viewed the Aboriginal Peoples as primitives or savages. Treaties were often ignored because the Europeans viewed themselves as superior to the Aboriginal Peoples, so their land could be taken without bothering with treaties. Many believed it was their duty to assimilate the Aboriginal Peoples into European religion and culture.

When Canada first became a nation, the government decided to assimilate Canada's Aboriginal Peoples into Canadian culture. This was to be done by making them abandon their native religious and cultural practices and join mainstream Canadian society. Essentially, the First Nations were treated as children in need of proper education and a firm hand. This treatment of the Aboriginal Peoples was formalized in the Indian Act of 1876.

Residential Schools

One method of assimilation was the residential school system. Under this system, aboriginal youth were to be educated in European culture, science, history, and religion, and aboriginal culture was to be gradually phased out.

Conditions at the schools were terrible. Aboriginal students were forced to attend and they were often removed from their families and housed in walled residences. If they spoke their native languages or practiced their own religion, they were beaten. They were not allowed to miss class, even if they were severely ill, and this contributed to the spread of diseases such as tuberculosis among the students. In several cases, students were subjected to sexual abuse.

These experiences disrupted and damaged the students, their families, and their communities. In 1998, the government acknowledged the excesses of the residential school system and began the process of reconciliation and resolution with those who had been forced to attend. In 2008, in an address that was broadcast nationally, Prime Minister Stephen Harper formally apologized for the creation of the residential school system.

WAR INTERNMENT CAMPS

During the First World War, Canadians whose ancestors had immigrated from enemy nations (Germany and the nations of the Austro-Hungarian Empire, especially Ukraine) were treated as enemy aliens. They were forced to register with the government, and approximately 5 000 people were imprisoned in internment camps. The detainees were often forced to work as labourers and had their property confiscated.

Much the same thing occurred during the Second World War after the Japanese attack on Pearl Harbor. Although the Japanese had attacked the United States, people of Japanese descent were treated more harshly in Canada than they were in the United States. Nearly 22 000 Japanese-Canadians were imprisoned. Their property was confiscated, and they were used as forced labour. Ironically, some of the interned citizens had fought for Canada during the First World War.

12.3.8   Evaluate the extent to which governments should promote individual and collective rights

RIGHTS AND FREEDOMS IN LIBERAL DEMOCRACIES

THE CANADIAN CHARTER OF RIGHTS AND FREEDOMS

The Canadian Charter of Rights and Freedoms is part of Canada's Constitution, which came into effect in 1982. It sets out the rights and freedoms that Canadian citizens are entitled to. These rights include the following:

- Fundamental freedoms (freedom of thought, freedom of religion, freedom of association, etc.)
- Democratic rights (right to vote, right to periodic elections, etc.)
- Mobility rights (right to move between Canada's provinces and territories)
- Legal rights (right to privacy, protection from cruel and unusual punishment, etc.)
- Equality rights (affirmation that all citizens are equal under the law)
- Other rights (language rights, multiculturalism, Aboriginal treaty rights, etc.)

The Supreme Court of Canada has final authority over interpretation of the charter.

The charter also includes a clause called the notwithstanding clause. This clause allows a provincial legislature to pass laws that may violate certain sections of the charter. The notwithstanding clause gives the provinces more say in their own affairs, but its use is not without limits. It can only be applied to fundamental freedoms, legal rights, and equality rights. Also, it can only be used where the provincial legislature has jurisdiction (legal power), so it cannot be used to change federal laws. Finally, citizens tend to take a negative view of having their rights violated, so a government that misuses the notwithstanding clause will pay for it at election time. Therefore, provincial governments tend to be cautious when using the notwithstanding clause.

THE QUEBEC CHARTER OF HUMAN RIGHTS AND FREEDOMS

The government of Quebec did not approve the Constitution Act of 1982, so it maintained its own bill of rights: the Quebec Charter of Human Rights and Freedoms. It is similar to the Canadian charter, but it also extends to economic and social rights, whereas Canada's charter covers civil and political rights. The Quebec charter came into effect in 1976. It is important to note that the Canada's charter takes precedence over Quebec's charter, even though Quebec did not approve the Constitution Act.

WAR MEASURES ACT

Liberal democracies, such as Canada, include laws that allow the government to suspend civil liberties during periods of crisis. For much of Canada's history, the emergency security law was the War Measures Act (1914). The act, when invoked, essentially transferred power to the Governor General of Canada, who acted on the advice of the cabinet. It allowed the Governor General to override much of the Charter of Rights and Freedoms and take a variety of illiberal actions: censorship, control over transportation and industry, confiscation of private property, and arrest, detention, or deportation without due process.

The government could only invoke the War Measures Act during times of war or insurrection. This occurred three times: for both World Wars and for the October Crisis. The October Crisis occurred when a group of militant Québécois nationalists called the Front de libération du Québec (FLQ) kidnapped a British diplomat and a provincial cabinet minister. During the World Wars, the War Measures Act was used to legalize the internment of enemy aliens; during the October Crisis, anyone expressing approval of the FLQ could be jailed on suspicion of belonging to the group.

The War Measures Act was replaced with the Emergencies Act in 1988. The key difference between the two acts is that the government must still act within the bounds of the Charter of Rights and Freedoms when invoking the Emergencies Act. The Governor General and the cabinet must also receive the approval of Parliament before declaring a state of emergency.

12.3.9 Evaluate the extent to which the principles of liberalism are viable in the context of contemporary issues

LIBERTY AND SECURITY

Liberal ideological values come under near-constant challenge. Liberal democracies often face difficult choices when presented with real-world problems

One of the responsibilities of the government is to protect its citizens from harm. Any nation is vulnerable, whether it be to war, disease, or terrorist attacks. Because they allow freedom of movement, liberal democracies are particularly vulnerable to the latter two. Infectious diseases can grow to become pandemics if they are not contained. In recent times, fears over severe acute respiratory syndrome (SARS) and avian influenza ("bird flu") have caused liberal democracies to make illiberal choices, such as restricting people's free movement and interfering with trade.

The problem of terrorism was brought home to North Americans on September 11, 2001, when the terrorist organization al-Qaida hijacked four commercial airliners. Two of the planes struck the twin towers of New York City's World Trade Center, completely destroying the buildings. A third plane caused heavy damage to the Pentagon, the headquarters of the United States Department of Defence. The fourth crashed in Pennsylvania as the passengers attemped to retake the plane from the terrorists.

Because of the attacks, all civilian air traffic was grounded for three days, and many flights were diverted to Mexico and Canada. Canada quickly launched Operation Yellow Ribbon to help coordinate the sudden, massive influx of air traffic. Canada shut down their airspace (except for necessary military and humanitarian flights) and received approximately 45 000 passengers who all needed food and shelter until the resolution of the crisis.

The United States declared a war on terrorism, and in October 2001, they passed the controversial USA PATRIOT Act. The act increased the power of law enforcement to search people's private records, detain and deport suspected terrorists, and monitor financial transactions. Some citizens were in favour of the USA PATRIOT Act and the extra security that it brought; others opposed it, as it violated several constitutionally guaranteed civil rights.

The Canadian government passed anti-terrorism legislation of its own—the Canadian Anti-Terrorism Act—but was widely criticized for the broad powers that the act gave to law enforcement, many of which violated the Charter of Rights and Freedoms. However, the Anti-Terrorism Act has not been widely used, and several of its provisions expired in 2007.

PRACTICE QUESTIONS—RELATED ISSUE 3

1. In Canada, consensus decision-making is used in
   A. Alberta
   B. Quebec
   C. Nunavut
   D. the Yukon

2. In practice, the government of the Russian Federation is
   A. a theocracy
   B. an oligarchy
   C. a democracy
   D. a one-party state

3. Collectivist economies are called
   A. control economies
   B. command economies
   C. communist economies
   D. cooperative economies

4. What is the boom-bust cycle?
   A. The alternating periods of economic prosperity and depression
   B. The tendency of the rich to get richer and the poor to stay poor
   C. A political theory about the rise and fall of governmental power
   D. A Marxist theory about the tendency of large corporations to fragment

5. In theory, which of the following statements about collectivist economies is **true**?
   A. No citizen is richer or poorer than another.
   B. There are no periods of economic depression.
   C. Citizens are rewarded in proportion to their efforts.
   D. Collectivist economies are weaker than free market economies.

6. Liberal democracies often react to serious crises by
   A. imposing special taxes
   B. suspending civil liberties
   C. taking direct control of the economy
   D. granting increased powers to the police

7. What type of economic system does Canada have?

    A. Mixed economy

    B. Collective economy

    C. Command economy

    D. Free market economy

8. In Canada, the citizens elect people to serve in the government on their behalf. This is known as

    A. direct democracy

    B. liberal democracy

    C. deliberative democracy

    D. representative democracy

9. What was the **main** purpose of the residential school system?

    A. To provide aboriginal children with free education

    B. To teach aboriginal children about their native culture

    C. To assimilate aboriginal children into European culture

    D. To help alleviate the social ills plaguing aboriginal communities

10. The October Crisis occurred when

    A. members of the Mohawk nation demanded the return of their traditional land

    B. a militant Québécois nationalist group engaged in kidnapping and other crimes

    C. the government cracked down on suspected terrorists after the attacks of September 11, 2001

    D. a large group of environmentalist protesters blockaded a logging camp in British Columbia

11. Which of the following ethnic groups was treated as an enemy alien in Canada during the First World War?

    A. Italian

    B. Russian

    C. Japanese

    D. Ukrainian

12. Which part of the Canadian Constitution deals with rights and freedoms?

    A. The Bill of Rights and Freedoms

    B. The Charter of Rights and Freedoms

    C. The Bill of Human Rights and Freedoms

    D. The Charter of Human Rights and Freedoms

13. When an infectious disease spreads throughout a nation or multiple nations, it is called
    A. an endemic

    B. a pandemic

    C. an epidemic

    D. a prosodemic

14. Which organization was responsible for the terrorist attacks of September 11, 2001?
    A. Hamas

    B. Al-Qaida

    C. Hezbollah

    D. Islamic Jihad

15. Which of the following groups of people had to wait the **longest** to receive full suffrage in Canada?
    A. Women

    B. The Inuit

    C. First Nations

    D. European men

Use the following information to answer the next question.

Statement I
Everyone is born free and equal.
Statement II
Everyone has the right to own property.
Statement III
Everyone has the right to life, liberty, and security.
Statement IV
Everyone has the right to equal pay for equal work.

16. Which of the given statements refers to the protection of human rights in the labour movement?
    A. Statement I

    B. Statement II

    C. Statement III

    D. Statement IV

Use the following information to answer the next question.

> • Land treaties
> • Residential schools
> • The 1969 White Paper
> • The Gradual Civilization Act

17. The given list contains examples of liberalism imposed on which group?

A. Women

B. First Nations

C. British royalty

D. European settlers

Use the following information to answer the next question.

Political Process
1. A question is presented to the group
2. Opinions are given
3. A response is agreed upon
4. Disagreements to the response are presented to the group
5. Modifications to the response are made
6. Discussions about the modified response occur
7. The process is repeated until a response agreed upon by all members is reached

18. The process outlined would **most likely** be used in which type of government?

A. Direct democracy

B. Representative democracy

C. Proportional representation

D. Consensus decision-making

19. At the federal level, the political process in Canada is **best** described as

A. authoritarian

B. a direct democracy

C. proportional representation

D. a representative democracy

Use the following information to answer the next question.

- A small, elite group of people hold the political power.
- Only one party is allowed to exist for elections and to form the government.
- The military overthrow the existing government and refuse to give up power.
- A law is created whereby only the sons and grandsons of one person are allowed to rule.

20. In which of the following types of government are the given characteristics primarily found?
    A. Authoritarian
    B. A direct democracy
    C. Proportional representation
    D. A representative democracy

Use the following information to answer the next two questions.

Sections 58 and 69 of Quebec's Charter of the French Language states that public signs, posters, and commercial advertising shall be only in French and only the French version of a business name may be used.

21. The given sections of Quebec's Charter of the French Language are in violation of
    A. local bylaw
    B. provincial legislation
    C. the Canadian Charter of Rights and Freedoms
    D. the Quebec Charter of Human Rights and Freedoms

22. The given sections of Quebec's Charter of the French Language place collective rights above

    A. social rights
    B. perceived rights
    C. economic rights
    D. individual rights

23. Today, a liberal democracy like Canada is most likely to suspend civil liberties when faced with which of the following issues?
    A. War
    B. Debt
    C. Pandemic
    D. Censorship

ANSWERS AND SOLUTIONS—PRACTICE QUESTIONS

1.	C	6.	B	11.	D	16.	D	21.	C
2.	B	7.	A	12.	B	17.	B	22.	D
3.	B	8.	D	13.	B	18.	D	23.	C
4.	A	9.	C	14.	B	19.	D		
5.	A	10.	B	15.	C	20.	A		

1. C

The territorial legislature of Nunavut uses a non-partisan, consensus decision-making model.

2. B

Although the Russian Federation operates as a democracy, real political power rests in the hands of a few wealthy and well-connected families. Therefore, in practice, the Russian Federation is an oligarchy.

Theocracy places political authority in the hands of religious figures. One-party states allow only one political party to exist and run for political office.

3. B

In collectivist societies, the economy is directly controlled by the government; such economies are known as command economies.

4. A

The boom-bust cycle is more formally called the business or economic cycle. Free market economies tend to follow a wave-like trend of increasing and decreasing economic power. The high points are boom periods; the low points are bust periods.

5. A

In theory, citizens in collectivist economies are economically equal, since the government redistributes wealth equitably among the citizens.

Although collectivist economies can soften the impact of a depression, they cannot eliminate them. Collectivist economies can be strong; the Soviet Union was once an economic powerhouse. Citizens are not rewarded in proportion to their efforts in collectivist economies.

6. B

In times of crisis, liberal democracies can legally suspend civil liberties in order to ensure the security of citizens. This can take many forms, such as banning of certain imports and declaring martial law.

7. A

Most liberal democracies, including Canada, combine elements of free market (capitalist) and command (collective) economic systems. This type of economy is known as a mixed economy.

8. D

Citizens in Canada elect representatives in the government. Therefore, Canada uses representative democracy.

Direct democracy is when citizens vote directly on laws and amendments. *Liberal democracy* is a term for any democracy based on liberal principles (rights and freedoms). Deliberative democracy is when the government gathers feedback from citizens to inform its decisions.

9. C

> The residential school system was established to force aboriginal children to adopt European culture.

10. B

> The October Crisis occurred in 1970, when a group known as the FLQ kidnapped a British diplomat and a Quebec cabinet minister. The FLQ wanted to make Quebec into a sovereign Marxist nation. This resulted in the third and last invocation of the War Measures Act.

11. D

> At the time of the First World War, Ukraine was a subject nation of the Austro-Hungarian Empire. The newly created War Measures Act stipulated that Canadians from "hostile nations" were to register with the government. Those considered particularly suspicious were held in internment camps. Although the act technically applied to Germans, Austrians, and other ethnicities from the Central Powers, Ukrainian-Canadians bore the brunt of the government's policy.

12. B

> The Canadian Charter of Rights and Freedoms is the part of the Constitution that provides citizens with guaranteed rights and freedoms.

13. B

> A pandemic is an infectious disease that spreads over a large area, often involving multiple nations.

An endemic disease is one that consistently appears in a particular area. An epidemic occurs when a disease is spreading faster than normal. A *prosodemic* disease is any disease that can be transmitted from one human directly to another.

14. B

> The attacks of September 11, 2001, were planned and carried out by al-Qaida, an organization that began as a group of anti-Soviet freedom fighters in Afghanistan.

Hamas and Hezbollah are politically powerful in Palestine and Lebanon, respectively; Canada, among other nations, has officially designated them as terrorist organizations. Islamic Jihad is an umbrella group for movements in Egypt, Palestine, and Lebanon; again, Canada considers the Islamic Jihad groups to be terrorist organizations.

15. C

> First Nations people did not receive full suffrage until 1960.

All Canadian citizens of European descent, both men and women, were given the right to vote federally in 1920. The Inuit gained the right to vote in 1950.

16. D

> Statement IV is about all people receiving equal pay for equal work. This human right is still a struggle for many people around the world, even in modern liberal and economically prosperous societies.

17. B

> The First Nations people in Canada had several liberal philosophies imposed on them. Residential schools, the original land treaties, the 1969 White Paper, and the Gradual Civilization Act were all liberal ideas that were being used to force the assimilation of First Nations people into Canadian society. Most First Nations people did not accept these ideas.

18. D

The given process is known as *consensus decision-making*. It involves a group of people that works toward unanimous agreement when finding solutions to problems

A *direct democracy* is rarely seen other than in smaller organizations, because it involves all members of a society voting on every issue and action, which would be too cumbersome for modern-day politics. A *representative democracy* is the type of government present in Canada. Citizens elect representatives from a party and the government is formed by the party with the largest number of elected representatives. *Proportional representation* is when citizens vote directly for a party and representatives are assigned based on the popular vote obtained by each party.

19. D

Canada has what is known as a representative democracy. Citizens elect representatives from a party and the government is formed by the party with the largest number of elected representatives.

An *authoritarian government* is led by one person or a small group of people who have no constitutional accountability to the people. The rights of individuals are ignored in favour of the power of the state. A *direct democracy* is rarely seen other than in smaller organizations, because it involves all members of a society voting on every issue and action, which would be too cumbersome for modern-day politics. *Proportional representation* is when citizens vote directory for a party and representatives are assigned based on the popular vote obtained by each party.

20. A

An authoritarian government is led by one person or a small group of people who have no constitutional accountability to the people. The rights of individuals are ignored in favour of the power of the state.

A *direct democracy* is rarely seen other than in smaller organizations, because it involves all members of a society voting on every issue and action, which would be too cumbersome for modern-day politics. A *representative democracy* is the type of government present in Canada. Citizens elect representatives from a party and the government is formed by the party with the largest number of elected representatives. *Proportional representation* is when citizens vote directly for a party and representatives are assigned based on the popular vote obtained by each party.

21. C

Sections 58 and 69 of Quebec's Charter of the French Language are in violation of the Canadian Charter of Rights and Freedoms.

22. D

The collective rights of the francophone community are being placed above citizen's individual rights.

23. C

The situation most likely to cause a suspension of civil liberties in present-day Canada would be a pandemic, as stipulated by the Emergencies Act of 1988.

UNIT TEST—RELATED ISSUE 3

1. For which of the following reasons are military dictatorships less common now than they were in the 20th century?

   A. They can no longer align themselves with more powerful nations.

   B. The United Nations works to prevent such dictatorships from arising.

   C. The increasing prevalence of democracy means fewer military coups.

   D. The United States is committed to helping overthrow such dictatorships.

2. Which of the following statements about traditional economies is **false**?

   A. They tend to be small-scale economies.

   B. They tend to be collectivist rather than individualist.

   C. They tend not to incorporate new practices or technologies.

   D. They comprise an insignificant portion of the global economy.

3. According to proponents of modern free market economics, the **main** role of the government should be to

   A. lower personal taxes

   B. lower corporate taxes

   C. set international tariffs

   D. regulate the money supply

4. What is the **main** vulnerability of a free market economy?

   A. Class warfare

   B. Risk of capital

   C. Boom-bust cycles

   D. Stock market crashes

5. How do command economies lessen the impact of economic depression?

   A. By nationalizing key industries

   B. By encouraging limited capitalism

   C. By taking control of the means of production

   D. By redistributing wealth equitably among the citizenry

6. One disadvantage of command economies is that they
   A. create economic imbalances
   B. eliminate individual incentive
   C. are vulnerable to boom-bust cycles
   D. are less efficient than free market economies

7. How does Canada help protect its citizens from boom-bust cycles?
   A. By increasing taxes
   B. By deregulating the economy
   C. By providing social programs
   D. By nationalizing key industries

8. In which of the following ways can a Canadian citizen participate in direct democracy?
   A. By voting on a referendum
   B. By running for public office
   C. By writing to a cabinet minister
   D. By obtaining a political party membership

9. Representative democracies must guard against which of the following political situations?
   A. Tyranny of the majority
   B. Weak minority governments
   C. Disenfranchisement of citizens
   D. Rise of totalitarian governments

10. What restrains majority governments in Canada from acting irresponsibly?
    A. They would become unpopular with voters.
    B. They are forbidden from doing so by the Constitution.
    C. The Governor General would intervene on behalf of the citizens.
    D. The Supreme Court of Canada would invalidate the government.

11. For what reason did aboriginal children attend residential schools?
    A. They were forced to do so under law.
    B. They were encouraged to do so by their elders
    C. They wanted to fit in with mainstream Canadian society.
    D. They saw the schools as an opportunity to better themselves.

12. Which of the following abuses did **not** occur in residential schools?
    A. Students were confined in prison-like residences.
    B. Students were sometimes subjected to sexual abuse.
    C. Students were punished for speaking their native tongue.
    D. Students were forced to attend classes unless they were seriously ill.

13. During the Second World War, Canadians of which ethnicity were treated as enemy aliens?
    A. Italian
    B. German
    C. Chinese
    D. Japanese

14. Which of the following statements regarding internment is **false**?
    A. The internees were used as forced labour.
    B. The internees were housed in concentration camps.
    C. The internees were forced to adopt European culture.
    D. The internees had their personal property confiscated.

15. Who has final authority of interpretation of the Canadian Charter of Rights and Freedoms?
    A. The cabinet
    B. The Governor General
    C. The houses of Parliament
    D. The Supreme Court of Canada

16. What is the **main** difference between Quebec's bill of rights and Canada's bill of rights?
    A. Quebec's bill of rights cannot be set aside during times of crisis.
    B. Quebec's bill of rights asserts Quebec's status as a distinct society.
    C. Quebec's bill of rights provides for socioeconomic rights and freedoms.
    D. Quebec's bill of rights has a section dealing with aboriginal rights and freedoms.

17. In Quebec, which bill of rights takes precedence: that of Quebec or that of Canada?
    A. Quebec, because they invoked the notwithstanding clause
    B. Quebec, because they did not accept the Constitution Act of 1982
    C. Canada, because Quebec approved the Charlottetown Accord of 1992
    D. Canada, because the Constitution Act of 1982 applies to all provinces

18. When invoked, the War Measures Act gave emergency authority and powers to the
    A. Queen
    B. prime minister
    C. Governor General
    D. minister of defence

19. Canada invoked its War Measures Act during which of the following events?
    A. The Oka Crisis
    B. The October Crisis
    C. The 9/11 terrorist attacks
    D. The Red River Resistance

20. What is the **main** difference between the War Measures Act and the Emergencies Act?
    A. The Emergencies Act forbids the government from conscripting citizens.
    B. The Emergencies Act contains specific measures against terrorist groups.
    C. The Emergencies Act does not supersede the Charter of Rights and Freedoms.
    D. The Emergencies Act allows the Governor General to assume control of the country.

21. Which of the following diseases has become a pandemic in recent years?
    A. BSE
    B. CHD
    C. AIDS
    D. SARS

22. What was the purpose of Operation Yellow Ribbon?
    A. To identify and monitor suspected terrorists
    B. To coordinate air traffic diverted from the United States
    C. To assist the United States in the invasion of Afghanistan
    D. To place the Canadian Air Force under temporary American command

23. The United States did **not** respond to the September 11 attacks by
    A. developing and passing the anti-terrorist USA PATRIOT Act
    B. declaring a war on terror—a warning to any nations harbouring terrorists
    C. clearing its airspace of all air traffic except military and humanitarian flights
    D. planning and initiating the invasion of Iraq and the ousting of Saddam Hussein

24. The USA PATRIOT Act gave law enforcement all of the following powers **except** the power to
    A. detain and deport suspected terrorists
    B. search the private information of suspected terrorists
    C. monitor the financial transactions of suspected terrorists
    D. physically coerce suspected terrorists into revealing information

25. Several sections of the USA PATRIOT Act were overturned because they were
    A. expensive
    B. impractical
    C. unnecessary
    D. unconstitutional

ANSWERS AND SOLUTIONS—UNIT TEST

1.	A	6.	B	11.	A	16.	C	21.	C
2.	D	7.	C	12.	D	17.	D	22.	B
3.	D	8.	A	13.	D	18.	C	23.	D
4.	C	9.	A	14.	C	19.	B	24.	D
5.	D	10.	A	15.	D	20.	C	25.	D

1. A

During the Cold War, a military dictatorship could seize or maintain power by aligning themselves ideologically with either the United States or the Soviet Union. They would receive support from the superpower, often in spite of human rights abuses. Today, a military dictatorship would not be sheltered by a superpower, and would have no international legitimacy.

2. D

Traditional economies employ 400 million people worldwide, making the traditional economy a significant contributor to the global economy.

3. D

Although proponents of free market economics support the reduction of taxes, they see the primary role of the government as regulator of the money supply. This allows the government to influence the supply side of the supply-demand dynamic and, in theory, ensure economic prosperity.

4. C

Unregulated free market economies go through cycles of boom and bust (prosperity and depression).

Class warfare is rarely a risk in a stable democracy. The risk of capital is essential to the free market. Stock market crashes can contribute to the bust phase of the boom-bust cycle, but they are not the only possible trigger.

5. D

Under a command economy, material wealth is redistributed as needed to the citizens.

Command economies nationalize (put under state control) all industries, not just key industries. If a command economy encouraged limited capitalism, it would essentially become a mixed economy. Taking control of the means of production allows some control over the boom-bust cycle, but it does not allow the government to alleviate economic depression.

6. B

In command economies, resources are redistributed equally among the citizens. This tends to eliminate individual incentive, since innovation and education do not significantly benefit individuals.

7. C

Canada provides employment insurance, skills upgrading, and other social programs aimed at helping citizens get through bust periods (periods of recession or depression).

Tax increases would only increase the hardship of bust periods. Economic deregulation, in which the government withdraws from economic involvement, would increase the severity of the boom-bust cycle. The nationalization of industries has little impact on boom-bust cycles.

8. A

A referendum is when the public is asked to vote directly on a particular law or amendment. In Canada, referendums are rare—only three have been held at the federal level.

Running for office, writing to a cabinet minister, and becoming a party member are all examples of participation in a representative democracy.

9. A

Because a political party can form a majority government (in which the party comprises over half of the total membership in the legislature or Parliament), they can, in theory, act without considering the needs or concerns of the minority. This would result in a tyranny of the majority.

Weak minority governments do occur, but can do little harm—representative democracies have mechanisms in place to remove such governments. The disenfranchisement (removal of voting power) of citizens seldom occurs in representative democracies because voting rights are constitutionally protected. The rise of totalitarian governments in democracies is exceedingly rare, since democracies tend to be stable and ideologically opposed to totalitarianism.

10. A

As long as a majority government does not violate the Constitution or the rule of law, it can legally do whatever it wants. However, Canadians have shown that they vote against a government that has acted irresponsibly like in case of the Airbus affair and the sponsorship scandal. Therefore, to win the next election, the ruling party (and the prime minister in particular) must act responsibly and avoid scandal.

11. A

For aboriginal children, attendance at residential schools was mandatory. A child's parents could be arrested if they kept the child at home. The residences themselves often resembled prison barracks, including measures to prevent children from escaping.

12. D

Students were not forced to attend classes even if they were seriously ill.

13. D

The attack on Pearl Harbor sparked fears in Canada that the Japanese would attack or invade the West Coast. Therefore, under the War Measures Act, Japanese-Canadians were forced to register with the government and were frequently subjected to internment.

14. C

The internees were not forced to adopt European culture, many had already done so. Their internment was based on ethnic or racial heritage, not culture.

The internees were used as forced labour and had their personal property confiscated. The internment camps were, in fact, concentration camps where people of a particular ethnicity are concentrated in one place.

15. D

The Supreme Court of Canada is Canada's highest judicial authority. If there is doubt as to whether a new law or amendment adheres to the charter, it is the Supreme Court that makes the final decision.

16. C

Quebec's charter provides social and economic rights not covered by the Canadian Charter of Rights and Freedoms.

17. D

Even though Quebec did not approve the Constitution Act of 1982, the act still passed. As a member of the Canadian federation, Quebec must abide by the Canadian Constitution, and that includes the Charter of Rights and Freedoms.

18. C

When invoked, the War Measures Act gave emergency authority to the Governor General of Canada, who would be advised by the federal cabinet.

19. B

Aside from the two World Wars, the only time that the Canadian government invoked the War Measures Act was during the October Crisis of 1970. The crisis occurred when a British diplomat and a Quebec politician were kidnapped by a militant separatist group called the FLQ.

The Oka Crisis and the 9/11 terrorist attacks occurred after the act was replaced; the Red River Resistance occurred before the act was created.

20. C

Under the Emergencies Act, the government (including law enforcement) must act within the bounds of the Canadian Charter of Rights and Freedoms during times of crisis.

21. C

AIDS (acquired immune deficiency syndrome) currently affects over 30 million people worldwide.

BSE (bovine spongiform encephalopathy, or "mad cow disease") and SARS (severe acute respiratory syndrome) were prevented from reaching pandemic levels by governments and international health organizations. CHD (coronary heart disease) is not an infectious disease.

22. B

In response to the 9/11 attacks, the United States closed its airspace, diverting civilian air traffic to Canada and Mexico. Canada received an unexpected and massive amount of air traffic. To coordinate the safe landing and deplaning of the passengers, they launched Operation Yellow Ribbon.

23. D

The invasion of Iraq was prompted by fears in the United States that Iraq was developing weapons of mass destruction.

24. D

Although the USA PATRIOT Act gave new powers to law enforcement, the use of physical coercion was not among them.

25. D

Certain sections of the act were deemed to violate citizens' constitutional rights and were overturned by the United States Supreme Court.

Related Issue 4

Should My Actions as a Citizen Be Shaped by an Ideology?

RELATED ISSUE 4

Table of Correlations		
Specific Expectation	**Practice Questions**	**Unit Test Questions**
By the end of this course, students will:		
12.4 Students will assess their rights, roles, and responsibilities as citizens		
12.4.4 explore the relationship between personal and collective world views and ideology	17	8
12.4.5 explore how ideologies shape individual and collective citizenship	1, 2, 3, 15	1, 2, 3, 4, 5, 6, 7, 9
12.4.6 analyze perspectives on the rights, roles, and responsibilities of the individual in a democratic society (respect for law and order, dissent, civility, political participation, citizen advocacy)	4, 5, 6, 7, 8	10, 11, 12, 13, 14, 15
12.4.7 analyze perspectives on the rights, roles, and responsibilities of the individual during times of conflict (humanitarian crises, civil rights movements, antiwar movements, McCarthyism, pro-democracy movements, contemporary examples)	9, 10, 11, 12, 13, 14, 16, 18	16, 17, 18, 19, 20, 21, 22, 23

RELATED ISSUE 4: SHOULD MY ACTIONS AS A CITIZEN BE SHAPED BY AN IDEOLOGY?

12.4.4   Explore the relationship between personal and collective worldviews and ideology

WORLDVIEWS

A worldview, as the name suggests, is the way in which a person or group views the world. It includes a view of other cultures in relation to one's own, the nature of one's own society, one's place in the world, and past events and how they have shaped the present. Today, travel and communication are easier and less expensive than ever. Consequently, individuals from different cultures who have different worldviews have increasingly come in contact with each other. Mainstream European and Canadian worldviews have developed over the past few centuries. For example, the mainstream attitude toward the rights of women, workers, and Aboriginal Peoples has changed dramatically, especially in the 20th century.

WORLDVIEWS AND IDEOLOGIES

Worldview and ideology are closely linked and influence one another greatly. For example, a staunch Québécois nationalist will likely have a worldview influenced by his or her ideology—especially concerning Quebec's place in the Canadian federation. A traveller to Africa might witness poverty and starvation and be influenced to adopt a humanitarian ideology.

Modern times have highlighted conflicting worldviews and ideologies. Consider the recent American efforts at installing liberal-democratic governments in nations such as Afghanistan and Iraq. An American nationalist might view these efforts with pride. However, an Arab nationalist might be enraged, viewing the changes as a violation of Arab sovereignty. Many citizens wonder whether the new regimes can endure, and others see the change in regime as a necessary step to ensuring the safety of Western democracies.

12.4.5   Explore how ideologies shape individual and collective citizenship

IDEOLOGY AND CITIZENSHIP

In liberal democracies, citizens must choose how they will participate in the shaping of their government. Many choose to adhere to the ideology of a political party—an ideologically based political group that seeks election for its members. In Canada, there are five prominent parties at the federal level.

Conservative Party of Canada

The Conservative Party of Canada was formed in 2003 with the amalgamation of the old Progressive Conservative party and the Canadian Alliance (formerly the Reform Party, a western-based conservative party that advocated political reform). The Progressive Conservative party favoured a progressive social approach (gradual social progress). The new Conservative Party is socially conservative and tends to oppose initiatives like same-sex marriage. The party has always been fiscally conservative and supports lower taxes, increased spending on military and law enforcement, and laissez-faire economics. It also advocates increased government transparency and accountability. The Conservative Party is nicknamed the "Tories".

Liberal Party of Canada

The Liberal Party was founded in 1867. It is generally known as a centrist party, seeking a middle ground between conservatism and socialism. Thus, the Liberal Party shares certain ideas with the Conservative Party, including increased military spending and balanced budgets. On the other hand, the Liberal Party is more inclined to support socially liberal policies and increased spending on social programs. In recent times, the Liberal Party has formed powerful majority governments, in part because of the splitting of the conservative vote between the Progressive Conservatives and the Canadian Alliance. The merger of the two parties and a major financial scandal (the Sponsorship Scandal) has eroded the Liberal Party's power considerably. The Liberal Party is nicknamed the "Grits".

New Democratic Party of Canada

The New Democratic Party was founded in 1961. It was originally a socialist party, but in recent years it has become increasingly moderate. Ideologically, it is still slightly left of centre, and it is socially and fiscally liberal. It supports the expansion of social welfare programs, workers' rights, minority rights, and increased taxes on corporations. It also agrees with some of the other parties on various issues, most notably the need to reform the Senate and maintain a balanced budget. The New Democratic Party has never formed the federal government, but it often has had enough seats to exert influence in the House of Commons, especially during minority governments.

The Bloc Québécois

The Bloc Québécois is based in Quebec and was founded in 1991. Its members promote Quebec's regional interests in the House of Commons and advocate increased sovereignty for that province (up to and including secession from Canada). In general, the party is socially liberal and fiscally conservative, and it often supports environmental and human rights causes. Despite its regional power base, the Bloc is influential enough to have formed the official Opposition (the party with the second-highest number of seats) after the 1993 federal election.

The Green Party of Canada

The Green Party was founded in 1983 and is primarily concerned with environmental causes. It is only recently (in 2004) that the Green party received enough of the popular vote to qualify for federal funding. Because the Green Party draws support from conservative, liberal, and socialist people who are concerned with the environment, it is difficult to pinpoint its location on the political spectrum. The Green Party believes the environment can be protected without overburdening the nation's finances. Furthermore, they predict that inaction on environmental matters will result in billions of dollars lost to cleanup in the future.

Party politics is at the core of Canadian government. Party loyalty is strictly enforced. Individual members of Parliament who violate party loyalty may be ejected from the party, and independent candidates seldom win elections. The parties determine the course they will take in regular caucuses (party meetings at which members try to achieve consensus on issues). Once the party has determined its direction, it presents a united front to the rest of the country.

12.4.6   Analyze perspectives on the rights, roles and responsibilities of the individual in a democratic society (respect for law and order, dissent, civility, political participation, citizen advocacy)

RIGHTS, ROLES, AND RESPONSIBILITIES IN A DEMOCRATIC SOCIETY

RESPONSIBILITIES OF CITIZENSHIP

Citizens in liberal democracies have certain basic responsibilities. First, they must pay their taxes. Second, they must obey their nation's laws, even if they are abroad. Finally, they must serve on a jury if selected to do so. Other responsibilities depend on the nation in question. For example, in Australia, all eligible citizens are required to vote. Other nations require a term of military service, but this is often limited to males only.

Many citizens feel that they also have moral responsibilities, such as voting, refraining from interfering with other citizens' rights, expressing national pride, and contributing to or working for charities. Although they may be influenced by social pressures, such things are generally up to the conscience of the individual.

DISSENT

Citizens in liberal democracies have the right to criticize the actions of their government. This criticism, when shared by a number of people, can turn into organized protests. As long as these protests are peaceful and orderly, they are perfectly legal. Protests take various forms, such as marches, assemblies, and boycotts. There are also more violent forms of protest, such as riots or direct attacks, but these are in no way protected under the Canadian Constitution or criminal law.

Some protesters employ civil disobedience—the simple refusal to obey laws that they consider unjust without resorting to violence or otherwise breaking the law. Thus, protesters may picket or blockade the entrance to a business they find offensive, refuse to pay a tax that they find unjust, or find other forms of disobedience. The largest act of civil disobedience in Canada occurred in 1993, when over 12 000 environmentalist protestors blockaded logging roads in Clayoquot Sound, British Columbia.

CIVILITY

The term *civility* covers a host of unwritten rules about social interaction in a community. Essentially, civil actions are those that society finds acceptable, polite, and inoffensive.

Civility is often defined not as a quality in and of itself, but as an avoidance of uncivil behaviour. A person who avoids rude or offensive behaviour, whether or not it is against the law, is being civil. Civility is important; it allows large numbers of people to live, work, and relax with one another. People who violate these rules are often subject to social pressure, which can be indirect or direct.

POLITICAL PARTICIPATION

Political participation involves far more than simply filling in a ballot every few years. There are a number of ways that Canadians can participate in politics. The most obvious way to participate is to seek public office. Canadians can also volunteer for a candidate's campaign; write letters or emails to MPs, MLAs, or city councillors; organize or attend political rallies; and join citizen advocacy groups.

CITIZEN ADVOCACY

Citizen advocacy groups are formed to effect political and social change. These groups focus the efforts of concerned citizens, enabling them to put more pressure on the government and to convey their message to the general public. Citizen advocacy groups often employ media campaigns, donation drives, and volunteer activists to help with their efforts.

Canada has several citizen advocacy groups dedicated to a variety of causes. One particularly prominent group is Mothers Against Drunk Driving (MADD). MADD seeks to increase public awareness about the dangers of drunk driving, and puts pressure on governments to take steps to address the problem. MADD also provides assistance to victims of drunk driving, trains victim service volunteers, and works with local police, ambulance, and firefighting services.

Citizen advocacy groups have an essential role in Canadian society: namely, to give a voice to people who are going unheard. Many citizen advocacy groups campaign for the rights of people with disabilities, the poor or the homeless, and other people who are often marginalized in mainstream society.

12.4.7   *Analyze perspectives on the rights, roles and responsibilities of the individual during times of conflict (humanitarian crises, civil rights movements, antiwar movements, McCarthyism, pro-democracy movements, contemporary examples)*

RIGHTS, ROLES, AND RESPONSIBILITIES DURING CONFLICT

HUMANITARIAN CRISES

Sometimes innocent people are caught up in disasters beyond their control and are left without the basic necessities for survival. Humanitarian crises can occur in the wake of natural disasters, wars, and pandemics. The international community responds to these crises by providing aid.

CRISIS: THE BOXING DAY TSUNAMI

On December 26, 2004, an extremely powerful earthquake beneath the Indian Ocean triggered a tsunami—a massive wave that radiated out from the earthquake's epicentre. The tsunami devastated the coastal regions and islands of the Indian Ocean, including countries such as India, Thailand, Sri Lanka, and Indonesia. When the wave subsided, over 200 000 people had lost their lives and around 10 million more were left homeless. Those in the affected areas were at risk of disease, given the lack of sanitation and clean water available. The international community responded with approximately $7 billion USD in aid.

CIVIL-RIGHTS MOVEMENTS

A civil-rights movement is a social and political movement on behalf of a particular group that is demanding legal equality. In Canada, civil-rights movements have been generally peaceful, but not without controversy.

In the United States, a major civil-rights movement began shortly after the end of the Second World War. Many American states openly discriminated against visible minority groups, especially people of African or Latin American descent. African Americans demanded equality before the law. The movement was largely led by Reverend Martin Luther King Jr., and it involved boycotts, protest marches, and rallies.

The civil-rights movement initially met with strong opposition but rapidly gathered momentum. The American public was shocked by images of unresisting black protesters being arrested, harassed, and beaten; they became increasingly sympathetic to the civil-rights movement. In the 1960s, during the presidencies of John F. Kennedy and Lyndon B. Johnson, the American government passed a number of civil- and political-rights acts.

Although these acts allowed African-Americans to begin active political participation and addressed many of the injustices they faced in American society, there still existed a strong undercurrent of racial tension. The late 1960s saw a number of violent riots, as poor urban African Americans reacted to the injustices and inequalities that still existed. Since then, race relations in the United States have steadily improved, but tension still remains in several major urban centres. In 2014, for example, African-Americans formed protests across the United States following the fatal shooting of a young African-American man by a police officer in Missouri.

ANTI-WAR MOVEMENTS

In the modern era, people have protested against war for a variety of different reasons, such as humanitarian reasons, religious reasons, and anti-globalization reasons. In recent times, anti-war movements have focussed on conflicts such as the Sudanese civil war, the United States-led invasion of Iraq, and the ongoing struggle between Israel and its neighbours. In Canada, over four million citizens belong to peace groups, which are coordinated by the Canadian Peace Alliance.

Anti-war movements tend to manifest themselves in acts of protest and civil disobedience as well as personal endeavours, including writing to members of Parliament and government ministers, signing petitions, and voting for anti-war candidates in elections.

McCARTHYISM

When a country is under threat, real or perceived, fear and suspicion can spread throughout the nation. There are examples of this throughout history, including the internment of those considered to be enemy aliens by the Canadian government during the Second World War. More recently, the terrorist attacks of September 11, 2001, had many living in fear of future attacks.

Immediately following the Second World War, American citizens were worried about the spread of communism and the possibility that Soviet spies and agitators were active in the United States. From 1945 to 1950, several incidents heightened this sense of fear, including the Soviet development of nuclear arms and a few high-profile espionage cases. In 1950, Wisconsin Senator Joseph McCarthy claimed that over 200 known communists were working in the American State Department.

There was no proof of these claims, but they terrified the American people. This fear spread through to the highest levels of government. The Federal Bureau of Investigation (FBI) doubled in size, and many unconstitutional or illegal practices were sanctioned by the government. Government officials (Senator McCarthy among them) held anti-communist hearings that investigated several facets of American government and society, most notably the armed forces and the film and television industries. Thousands of careers were destroyed and lives ruined by unsubstantiated accusations of communist activity.

The anti-communist hysteria and baseless accusations came to be known as McCarthyism, and from its outset, there was opposition to it. Many Americans were disgusted by the abuses that were permitted (or encouraged) during this time. Eventually, there was a massive media backlash against McCarthy and those who used similar scare tactics. The Supreme Court also put a stop to the unconstitutional practices.

Today, the term *McCarthyism* refers to any use in politics of baseless accusations of treason or disloyalty.

PRO-DEMOCRACY MOVEMENTS

The world has become increasingly democratic since the end of the Second World War. Much of this has to do with the decolonization of overseas empires (especially in Africa and India). However, several decolonized nations soon fell to totalitarian dictatorships. The collapse of the Soviet Union sparked pro-democracy movements throughout its constituent nations and satellite states. Democracy is now the world's dominant political ideology although many regions, such as Africa and Central and South America, are still struggling with dictatorships or unstable democracies.

SOLIDARITY

One of the best-known pro-democracy movements in the former Soviet bloc arose in Poland in 1980. It centred on a labour union movement called Solidarity, which was led by Lech Walesa. Despite the repression of the local Communist government, Walesa and Solidarity coordinated strikes around Poland throughout the 1980s. Eventually, the government agreed to allow partially free elections in 1989, and Solidarity's triumph was astounding: they won every seat in the lower house for which they were eligible and 99 of the 100 available seats in the senate.

Solidarity's victory meant the end of communist rule in Poland and inspired other Warsaw Pact nations to push for democracy. Not long after, the Communist Party of Hungary dissolved itself, but not before passing sweeping pro-democracy reforms. The governments of Czechoslovakia, Bulgaria, and East Germany collapsed under massive popular pro-democracy movements, and the government of Romania was violently overthrown. The movement soon spread to the Soviet Union itself, and just over two years after Solidarity's victory, the Soviet Union was formally dissolved.

PRACTICE QUESTIONS— RELATED ISSUE 4

1. Which two parties united to form the Conservative Party of Canada?
    A. The Progressive Conservative party and the Reform party
    B. The Progressive Conservative party and the Social Credit party
    C. The Progressive Conservative party and the Canadian Alliance party
    D. The Progressive Conservative party and the Co-operative Commonwealth Federation

2. For which of the following reasons is the Liberal Party of Canada seen as Canada's "centrist" party?
    A. They support a strong central government.
    B. They are neither conservative nor socialist.
    C. They derive most of their votes from Central Canada
    D. They traditionally sit in the centre of the House of Commons.

3. The Green Party of Canada is **primarily** concerned with
    A. workers' rights
    B. economic reform
    C. anti-globalization
    D. environmental protection

4. Which of the following duties is **not** required of citizens in Canada?
    A. Jury duty
    B. Military service
    C. Payment of taxes
    D. Obedience of the law

5. One example of a moral responsibility is
    A. voting
    B. jury duty
    C. paying taxes
    D. obeying the law

6. Which of the following forms of protest is **illegal**?
    A. Riots
    B. Rallies
    C. Marches
    D. Boycotts

7. In Canada, civility is **primarily** enforced through
   A. social pressure
   B. monetary fines
   C. codes of conduct
   D. police enforcement

8. What is the **primary** role of citizen advocacy groups?
   A. To lobby the government for favourable legislation
   B. To enforce civility through collective social pressure
   C. To collect money and recruit volunteers in order to help others
   D. To fight for rights or recognition of persons who are going unheard

9. Which of the following natural disasters struck the Indian Ocean and the surrounding regions in December 2004?
   A. A tornado
   B. A tsunami
   C. A severe hurricane
   D. A volcanic eruption

10. In Canada, the peace movement is **mostly** coordinated by
    A. Canadians United for Peace
    B. the Canadian Peace Alliance
    C. Canadians for National Peace
    D. the Canadian United Peace Movement

11. Which of the following incidents did **not** contribute to the American anti-communist hysteria of the 1950s?
    A. Photographs of nuclear missile bases in Cuba
    B. Nuclear weapons testing by the Soviet Union
    C. The public speeches of Senator Joseph McCarthy
    D. The discovery of Soviet spies in the United States

12. In general, the nations of the world have become increasingly
    A. socialist
    B. autocratic
    C. totalitarian
    D. democratic

13. Which of the following regions is **least** democratic?

   A. Southeast Asia

   B. Central Europe

   C. Eastern Europe

   D. Central America

14. Who was the leader of the Solidarity movement in Poland in the 1980s?

   A. Artur Boruc

   B. Lech Walesa

   C. Waclaw Kuchar

   D. Stanislaw Maczek

15. The economic freedom of classical liberalism and the social responsibility of modern liberalism are most at odds when contrasting

   A. social programs and welfare programs

   B. consumerism and social programs

   C. capitalism and consumerism

   D. collectivism and socialism

Use the following information to answer the next two questions.

Speaker I

I obey the laws and expect others to do the same.

Speaker II

I believe in my right to protest and disobey laws that I consider unjust, hoping to bring about change.

Speaker III

I believe we all have the duty to participate in our nation, including voting and serving jury duty.

Speaker IV

I believe that for large numbers of people to live together, we each must respect common decency and conduct ourselves appropriately.

---

16. Which speaker is most likely to have participated in the 1993 Clayoquot Sound protest?

   A. Speaker I

   B. Speaker II

   C. Speaker III

   D. Speaker IV

17. Which speaker places a high value on civility in society?

    A. Speaker I

    B. Speaker II

    C. Speaker III

    D. Speaker IV

Use the following information to answer the next question.

- The internment of Japanese Canadians during the Second World War

- The fear of certain groups of people after the September 11 terrorist attacks

- The fears of the spread of communism in the United States during the Cold War

18 Today, the given list would best be described by the term

    A. anti-war movements

    B. McCarthyism

    C. extremism

    D. liberalism

ANSWERS AND SOLUTIONS—PRACTICE QUESTIONS

1.	C	5.	A	9.	B	13.	D	17.	D
2.	B	6.	A	10.	B	14.	B	18.	B
3.	D	7.	A	11.	A	15.	B		
4.	B	8.	D	12.	D	16.	B		

1. C

The Progressive Conservatives and the Canadian Alliance united in 2003. The Canadian Alliance grew out of the Reform party, a chiefly western-based conservative movement.

The Social Credit party, another conservative movement, was largely defunct by the mid-1970s.
The Co-operative Commonwealth Federation is the predecessor of the New Democratic Party.

2. B

The Liberal Party of Canada has positioned itself politically between the Conservative Party and the more socialist New Democratic Party. This means that most people place the Liberal Party in the centre of the traditional political spectrum.

3. D

The Green Party of Canada is an environmentalist party. Its members believe environmental protection is realistic, practical, and can be done without harming the economy.

4. B

Canadian citizens are not legally required to serve a term in the military reserves.

This duty is required in some liberal democracies, such as Israel and Poland.

5. A

Many Canadians feel that citizens have a moral obligation to vote in elections and that if a citizen does not do so, they will lose the moral right to complain about the government.

Citizens are legally required to serve on juries when selected, to pay their taxes, and to obey the law.

6. A

Disorganized and violent protests (riots) are illegal.

Organized and peaceful protests such as rallies, marches, and boycotts are legal.

7. A

Social pressure is the primary means of ensuring that people are civil.

Only in extreme cases would fines or police be involved, which usually means a law has been broken.

8. D

The primary role of citizen advocacy groups is to advocate for persons who are going unheard: those who have been marginalized by society, those who do not have the right to vote (children), or those who have passed away.

9. B

On Boxing Day in 2004, a tsunami (a powerful wave caused by an underwater earthquake) slammed into the coasts and islands of the Indian Ocean, claiming well over 200 000 lives.

10. B

The Canadian Peace Alliance is an umbrella organization, which is a loose union of many different peace groups.

11. A

Missile bases were not discovered in Cuba until 1962, when the hysteria had largely died down.

12. D

Between the decolonization that followed the Second World War and the collapse of communism in Eastern Europe, the world has become increasingly democratic.

13. D

Many Central American nations are dictatorships.

The countries in central Europe, southeast Asia, and eastern Europe are primarily democratic.

14. B

Lech Walesa, an electrician by trade, led the Solidarity movement in the 1980s.

Artur Boruc is a soccer goalkeeper. Waclaw Kuchar was an Olympic athlete who excelled at many sports, and Stanislaw Maczek was a general during the Second World War.

15. B

The economic freedom of classical liberalism and the social responsibility of modern liberalism are most at odds when contrasting consumerism and social programs.

16. B

Speaker II is most likely to have participated in the 1993 Clayoquot Sound protest. This speaker believes in the right to protest and disobey laws that are considered unjust.

17. D

Speaker IV places a high value on civility in society. He or she believes that for society to function properly, common decency, respect, and appropriate conduct are necessary.

18 B

Senator Joe McCarthy was responsible for the movement to uncover and persecute those with possible or perceived ties to communism in the United States after the Second World War. His claims lacked proper evidence and resulted in widespread fear and discrimination. The term *McCarthyism* is still used today when there are concerns and discrimination based on possible or perceived connections to organizations or ideologies, such as terrorism.

UNIT TEST—RELATED ISSUE 4

1. The Conservative Party would **least likely** support increased
   A. corporate taxes
   B. law enforcement
   C. military spending
   D. government transparency

2. The New Democratic Party would **most likely** agree with the Conservative party on the need for
   A. a reformed Senate
   B. a stronger military
   C. higher corporate taxes
   D. environmental protection

3. Which of the following statements about the Bloc Québécois is **true**?
   A. The Bloc Québécois is socially and fiscally liberal.
   B. The Bloc Québécois is socially and fiscally conservative.
   C. The Bloc Québécois is socially conservative and fiscally liberal.
   D. The Bloc Québécois is socially liberal and fiscally conservative.

4. Which of the following political parties was **most recently** founded?
   A. The Green party
   B. The Liberal party
   C. The Bloc Québécois
   D. The New Democratic Party

5. Which of the following nicknames refers to the Conservative party?
   A. The Grits
   B. The Blues
   C. The Tories
   D. The Whigs

6. Which of the following initiatives would a Bloc Québécois member be **least likely** to support?
   A. Funding trade missions to promote Canadian businesses abroad
   B. Sending emergency aid to civilians in a war-torn African nation
   C. Reforming the House of Commons so that each province has an equal number of seats
   D. Providing tax incentives for industries to lower their pollution emissions to meet Kyoto targets

Use the following information to answer the next three questions.

Four Canadian citizens were asked if the government should raise taxes on corporations.

Speaker I

If corporate taxes were raised, then the government could lower citizens' taxes. This would mean that citizens would have more to spend, which would help stimulate the economy. However, it is important not to interfere too much; corporations are in business for a reason, and we do not want to take away their incentive.

Speaker II

I think the government should leave corporate taxes as they are. If we raise corporate taxes, corporations will pull up stakes and move their operations to a more business-friendly nation. That would mean lost tax income and fewer jobs for Canadians and the economy would be devastated.

Speaker III

Raising corporate taxes would be a good idea. Corporations benefit from government help with programs such as start-up incentives and assisted loans. A lot of them get tax breaks. Why should they not be made to pay their fair share instead? The government could use the extra revenue to help those in need.

Speaker IV

I think corporations that use up a lot of resources or create a lot of pollution should bear more of the tax burden. This country belongs to all Canadians, and the worst polluters should be made to pay for the harm they do to the environment.

---

7. Which speaker **most likely** belongs to the Liberal party?
   A. Speaker I
   B. Speaker II
   C. Speaker III
   D. Speaker IV

8. Which of the following issues do the speakers **not** address?
   A. Socialism
   B. Sovereignty
   C. Environmentalism
   D. Laissez-faire economics

9. Speaker II is **least likely** to belong to which of the following political parties?
   A. The Green party
   B. The Bloc Québécois
   C. The Conservative party
   D. The New Democratic Party

Four Canadians were asked what they would change about Canadian society.

Speaker I

I think that many citizens need to be more considerate of other people. People are out there driving like maniacs, listening to their music so loud it hurts people's ears, smoking in public places, littering … the list goes on and on. I guess there is no law against being inconsiderate, but that does not mean you should be.

Speaker II

Canadian citizens need to show a little national pride. As far as I am concerned, Canada is the best county in the world, and I am not afraid to show it. There is no harm in getting out there and waving the flag once in a while, and not just on Canada Day.

Speaker III

Although Canada is pretty good at taking care of those in need, charity is still important. A tiny fraction of your time or money can make all the difference in the world to someone who is ill, lonely, or hungry. If we all pitched in to help one another, we could make Canada a place where no one suffers needlessly.

Speaker IV

One thing that really gets on my nerves is people who complain about taxes. Taxes benefit everyone. They provide money to pave the roads, clean the streets, and maintain the parks, among other things. How else are our children going to get a quality education? How else are we going to maintain our military? Personally, I have no problem at all paying taxes.

10. All the speakers are concerned with moral responsibilities **except** for speaker

    A. Speaker I

    B. Speaker II

    C. Speaker III

    D. Speaker IV

11. Which speaker's views concern citizens' rights?

    A. Speaker I

    B. Speaker II

    C. Speaker III

    D. Speaker IV

12. In expressing their views, all four speakers are trying to change the behaviour of others through

    A. social pressure

    B. humanitarianism

    C. emotional appeal

    D. nationalist appeal

13. Which of the following statements about civil disobedience is **true**?

A. Civil disobedience is non-violent.

B. Boycotts are a form of civil disobedience.

C. Protesters rarely resort to civil disobedience.

D. Civil disobedience rarely involves illegal activity.

14. Which of the following acts of civil disobedience is the **largest** in Canada's history?

A. The Oka Crisis (1990)

B. The Conscription Crisis (1944)

C. The Elaho Valley protest (1999)

D. The Clayoquot Sound protest (1993)

15. In general, for which of the following reasons is civility important to a community?

A. It protects private property from destruction and theft.

B. It allows large numbers of people to live together peacefully.

C. It allows parents to pass their beliefs and morals to their children.

D. It ensures that no one in the community is impolite to anyone else.

16. The **primary** leader of the civil-rights movement in the United States was

A. Malcolm X

B. Sojourner Truth

C. Stokely Carmichael

D. Martin Luther King Jr.

17. Which of the following ideologies is **least likely** to be linked to an anti-war movement?

A. Pacifism

B. Humanitarianism

C. Environmentalism

D. Anti-globalization

18. If a politician is said to be practising McCarthyism, what behaviour is he or she engaging in?

A. Exploiting people's fears of communism for political gain

B. Accusing opponents of treason or disloyalty without proof

C. Fighting against any possible infiltration by hostile ideologies

D. Inventing stories of imminent danger to influence public opinion

19. In recent times, which of the following events has contributed **most** to increased democratization?

    A. Regime changes in the Middle East

    B. The decolonization of the African continent

    C. The collapse of communism in eastern Europe

    D. The overthrow of dictatorships in Central America

20. What is the world's **dominant** political ideology?

    A. Socialism

    B. Democracy

    C. Communism

    D. Totalitarianism

21. How did Solidarity gain control of the Polish government?

    A. They were voted in democratically.

    B. They seized control in a violent coup.

    C. They took over after the Communist government fled.

    D. They were granted power by Soviet General Secretary Gorbachev.

22. What is the **main** significance of Solidarity's victory in Poland?

    A. It signalled the end of Communist rule in Poland.

    B. It inspired a wave of pro-democracy movements in other Warsaw Pact nations.

    C. It was the first time that a free and fair election was held in a Warsaw Pact nation.

    D. It demonstrated that communism was extremely unpopular in Warsaw Pact nations.

23. Which of the following statements about the Warsaw Pact pro-democracy movements is **true**?

    A. The government of Czechoslovakia was violently overthrown.

    B. The pro-democracy movement spread into the Soviet Union itself.

    C. NATO provided economic backing for the pro-democracy movements.

    D. The Soviet military was unable to quell the pro-democracy movements.

ANSWERS AND SOLUTIONS—UNIT TEST

1.	A	6.	C	11.	A	16.	D	21.	A
2.	A	7.	A	12.	A	17.	C	22.	B
3.	D	8.	B	13.	A	18.	B	23.	B
4.	C	9.	D	14.	D	19.	C		
5.	C	10.	D	15.	B	20.	B		

1. A

The Conservative party supports laissez-faire economics, so it would not be in favour of high taxes on corporations.

2. A

Both the New Democratic Party and the Conservative party support Senate reform; as it stands, senators are appointed by the Governor General (based on the prime minister's recommendations).

3. D

The Bloc Québécois is socially liberal and fiscally conservative.

4. C

The Bloc Québécois was founded in 1991.

Of the other parties given, the Liberal party is the oldest (1867), followed by the New Democratic Party (1961) and the Green party (1983).

5. C

The Conservative party is often referred to as the Tories, particularly in the media.

The term *Grits* refers to the Liberal party. The term *Whig* used to refer to the Liberal party as well, but it is now used in Britain more often than in Canada. The Conservative party uses blue in its campaign signs, but they are not referred to as the Blues.

6. C

Because of its high population, Quebec would lose a great deal of political power if each province was given an equal number of seats. This would be unacceptable to a Bloc Québécois member.

7 A

Of all the speakers, Speaker I is the most moderate, seeking a balance between corporate taxation and individual taxation. The speaker's viewpoint is most in line with that of the Liberal party.

8. B

None of the speakers are particularly concerned with sovereignty (political independence).

Speaker III wants the government to use the tax revenue for social programs (a socialist standpoint). Speaker IV is concerned about the environment. Speakers I and II both stress the importance of minimal government interference in the economy.

9. D

The New Democratic Party supports higher corporate taxes, and Speaker II clearly does not.

Both the Conservative party and the Bloc Québécois are fiscally conservative, so they would agree with Speaker II. The Green party draws its membership from all over the political spectrum, so it is possible to have a fiscally conservative Green party member.

10. D

Speaker IV is concerned with taxes, which are a legal responsibility, not a moral responsibility.

11. A

Speaker I is essentially saying that people should respect one another's rights: this includes the moral right to be treated with consideration and respect, in addition to the rights that are guaranteed in the Constitution (legally protected), .

12 A

Social pressure is the attempt to sway people without direct coercion (e.g., laws, physical threats, or ultimatums). All four speakers exert social pressure.

13 A

One of the key components of civil disobedience is non-violent resistance.

Protesters may disobey the law, but the use of violent means would detract from the morality of their cause. Boycotts are forms of protest, not civil disobedience. Civil disobedience involves refusing to obey specific laws as a form of protest, but it does not involve violence. Civil disobedience is not common on a large scale, but it is frequently practiced by individual protesters or small groups.

14. D

Over 12 000 protesters were involved in the Clayoquot Sound protest; this is a far greater number than at the Elaho Valley protest.

Although the Oka Crisis started as civil disobedience, it escalated into a violent conflict. The Conscription Crisis involved a small mutiny, which was an act of military, not civil, disobedience.

15. B

In a way, civility is the glue that binds communities together. Because everyone in a community has more or less the same idea of what constitutes civil behaviour, they can live together without too much friction.

It cannot guarantee that everyone will act civilly, but social pressure will tend to keep individuals in line with mainstream civil behaviour.

16. D

The leader of the civil-rights movement was Martin Luther King Jr., a Baptist minister who believed in non-violent resistance.

Malcolm X was a Muslim minister known for his blunt indictments of America's treatment of African Americans. He advocated complete separation of whites and blacks into distinct nations. Sojourner Truth was a key figure in both the anti-slavery and women's suffrage movements in the late 19th century. Stokely Carmichael was a prominent member of the Black Panther movement.

17. C

Although warfare undoubtedly damages the environment, the focus of protest during times of war is about political and social injustice as well as the loss of human lives.

18. B

Today, McCarthy's name is synonymous with baseless accusations of treason and disloyalty.

19. **C**

All the former Soviet bloc nations and the constituent nations of the Soviet Union itself have become democracies.

In the Middle East, regime changes have only occurred in Afghanistan and Iraq, and those new democracies are still unstable. The decolonization of Africa did help some states achieve democracy, but many became totalitarian states. In Central America, if a dictatorship is overthrown, it is generally replaced with another dictatorship.

20. **B**

With the collapse of the Soviet Union and the democratization of eastern Europe, more nations are ruled democratically than by any other system of government.

21. **A**

Solidarity's triumph in the semi-free elections of 1989 was absolute; they won all but one seat in the 100-seat senate and every seat in the lower house for which they were eligible.

22. **B**

Solidarity's victory was the spark that ignited pro-democracy movements throughout the Soviet bloc, and it was one of the direct causes of the collapse of a world superpower.

Solidarity's victory did signal the end of communism in Poland, but the effect it had on other nations is more significant in global terms. It was not the first time a free and fair election was held in a Warsaw Pact nation because the election in Poland was far from free: Solidarity was only allowed to run for 35% of the seats in Poland's lower house of parliament. Finally, the election demonstrated the unpopularity of communism only in Poland. Other nations, such as Czechoslovakia and Hungary, had already tried to escape Soviet rule, but their attempts were crushed by the Soviet military.

23. **B**

In the wake of the successful pro-democracy movements in the satellite states, the constituent nations of the Soviet Union began to follow suit; this ended in the formal breakup of the Soviet Union in 1991.

The government of Czechoslovakia was not violently overthrown; it lost power because of massive popular resistance. Neither NATO nor the Soviet Union interfered in the pro-democracy movements.

KEY Strategies for Success on Tests

KEY STRATEGIES FOR SUCCESS ON TESTS

AN OVERVIEW OF THE TEST

This section is all about the skills and strategies you need to be successful on the Alberta Social Studies 30-1 Diploma Examination. It is designed for you to use together with your classroom learning and assignments.

FINDING OUT ABOUT THE TEST

Here are some questions you may wish to discuss with your teacher to help you prepare for the Social Studies 30-1 Diploma Examination:

1.	What is the format of the examination?	The examination has two parts: Part A: Written Response and Part B: Multiple-Choice. Each part is worth 50% of the total diploma examination.
2.	What do I need to know to do well on the assessment?	Part A is made up of two assignments: Assignment I—Source Interpretation and Assignment II—Position Paper. Part B consists of 60 multiple-choice questions.
3.	How important is this test to my final grade?	This examination is worth 30% of your final grade.

Having a good understanding of effective test taking skills can help you do well on the test. Being familiar with the question format may help you in preparing for quizzes, unit tests, or year-end tests.

THINGS TO CONSIDER WHEN TAKING A TEST

It is normal to feel anxious before you write a test. You can manage this anxiety by using the following strategies:

- Think positive thoughts. Imagine yourself doing well on the test.

- Make a conscious effort to relax by taking several slow, deep, controlled breaths. Concentrate on the air going in and out of your body.

- Before you begin the test, ask questions if you are unsure of anything.

- Jot down key words or phrases from any instructions your teacher gives you.

- Look over the entire test to find out the number and kinds of questions on the test.

- Read each question closely, and reread if necessary.

- Pay close attention to key vocabulary words. Sometimes, these words are **bolded** or *italicized*, and they are usually important words in the question.

- If you are putting your answers on an answer sheet, mark your answers carefully. Always print clearly. If you wish to change an answer, erase the mark completely, and ensure that your final answer is darker than the one you have erased.

- Use highlighting to note directions, key words, and vocabulary that you find confusing or that are important to answering the question.

- Double-check to make sure you have answered everything before handing in your test.

- When taking tests, students often overlook the easy words. Failure to pay close attention to these words can result in an incorrect answer. One way to avoid this is to be aware of these words and to underline, circle, or highlight them while you are taking the test.

- Even though some words are easy to understand, they can change the meaning of the entire question, so it is important that you pay attention to them. Here are some examples.

all	always	most likely	probably	best	not
difference	usually	except	most	unlikely	likely

Example

1. During the race, Susan is **most likely** feeling
    A. sad
    B. weak
    C. scared
    D. determined

HELPFUL STRATEGIES FOR ANSWERING MULTIPLE-CHOICE QUESTIONS

A multiple-choice question gives you some information and then asks you to select an answer from four choices. Each question has one correct answer. The other choices are distractors, which are incorrect. The following strategies can help you when answering multiple-choice questions:

- Quickly skim through the entire test. Find out how many questions there are, and plan your time accordingly.

- Read and reread questions carefully. Underline key words, and try to think of an answer before looking at the choices.

- If there is a graphic, look at the graphic, read the question, and go back to the graphic. Then, you may want to underline the important information from the question.

- Carefully read the choices. Read the question first and then each choice that goes with it.

- When choosing an answer, try to eliminate those choices that are clearly wrong or do not make sense.

- Some questions may ask you to select the best answer. These questions will always include words like *best*, *most appropriate*, or *most likely*. All of the choices will be correct to some degree, but one of the choices will be better than the others in some way. Carefully read all four choices before choosing the answer you think is the best.

- If you do not know the answer, or if the question does not make sense to you, it is better to guess than to leave it blank.

- Do not spend too much time on any one question. Make a mark (*) beside a difficult question, and come back to it later. If you are leaving a question to come back to later, make sure you also leave the space on the answer sheet, if you are using one.

- Remember to go back to the difficult questions at the end of the test; sometimes, clues are given throughout the test that will provide you with answers.

- Note any negative words like *no* or *not*, and be sure your answer fits the question.

- Before changing an answer, be sure you have a very good reason to do so.

- Do not look for patterns on your answer sheet, if you are using one.

HELPFUL STRATEGIES FOR ANSWERING WRITTEN-RESPONSE QUESTIONS

A written response requires you to respond to a question or directive indicated by words such as *explain*, *predict*, *list*, *describe*, *show your work*, *solve*, or *calculate*. The following strategies can help you when answering written-response questions:

- Read and reread the question carefully.

- Recognize and pay close attention to directing words such as *explain*, *show your work*, and *describe*.

- Underline key words and phrases that indicate what is required in your answer, such as *explain*, *estimate*, *answer*, *calculate*, or *show your work*.

- Write down rough, point-form notes regarding the information you want to include in your answer.

- Think about what you want to say, and organize information and ideas in a coherent and concise manner within the time limit you have for the question.

- Be sure to answer every part of the question that is asked.

- Include as much information as you can when you are asked to explain your thinking.

- Include a picture or diagram if it will help to explain your thinking.

- Try to put your final answer to a problem in a complete sentence to be sure it is reasonable.

- Reread your response to ensure you have answered the question.

- Ask yourself if your answer makes sense.

- Ask yourself if your answer sounds right.

- Use appropriate subject vocabulary and terms in your response

TEST PREPARATION COUNTDOWN

If you develop a plan for studying and test preparation, you will perform well on tests.

Here is a general plan to follow seven days before you write a test.

COUNTDOWN: 7 DAYS BEFORE THE TEST

1. Use "Finding Out about the Test" to help you make your own personal test preparation plan.

2. Review the following information:

    – Areas to be included on the test

    – Types of test items

    – General and specific test tips

3. Start preparing for the test at least seven days before the test. Develop your test preparation plan, and set time aside to prepare and study.

COUNTDOWN: 6, 5, 4, 3, 2 DAYS BEFORE THE TEST

1. Review old homework assignments, quizzes, and tests.

2. Rework problems on quizzes and tests to make sure you still know how to solve them.

3. Correct any errors made on quizzes and tests.

4. Review key concepts, processes, formulas, and vocabulary.

5. Create practice test questions for yourself, and answer them. Work out many sample problems.

COUNTDOWN: THE NIGHT BEFORE THE TEST

1. Use the night before the test for final preparation, which includes reviewing and gathering materials needed for the test before going to bed.

2. Most importantly, get a good night's rest, and know you have done everything possible to do well on the test.

TEST DAY

1. Eat a healthy and nutritious breakfast.

2. Ensure you have all the necessary materials.

3. Think positive thoughts, such as "I can do this," "I am ready," and "I know I can do well."

4. Arrive at your school early, so you are not rushing, which can cause you anxiety and stress.

SUMMARY OF HOW TO BE SUCCESSFUL DURING A TEST

You may find some of the following strategies useful for writing a test:

- Take two or three deep breaths to help you relax.

- Read the directions carefully, and underline, circle, or highlight any important words.

- Look over the entire test to understand what you will need to do.

- Budget your time.

- Begin with an easy question or a question you know you can answer correctly rather than follow the numerical question order of the test.

- If you cannot remember how to answer a question, try repeating the deep breathing and physical relaxation activities. Then, move on to visualization and positive self-talk to get yourself going.

- When answering questions with graphics (pictures, diagrams, tables, or graphs), look at the question carefully, and use the following steps:

  1. Read the title of the graphic and any key words.

  2. Read the test question carefully to figure out what information you need to find in the graphic.

  3. Go back to the graphic to find the information you need.

- Write down anything you remember about the subject on the reverse side of your test paper. This activity sometimes helps to remind you that you do know something and are capable of writing the test.

- Look over your test when you have finished, and double-check your answers to be sure you did not forget anything.

MULTIPLE-CHOICE OVERVIEW

The multiple-choice portion of the Diploma Exam is worth 50% of the total Diploma Examination mark. This section consists of 60 multiple-choice questions. Questions in this part of the exam are based on the key issues, related issues, and specific outcomes in the Alberta Social Studies Program of Studies. In this section of the test, you must apply your knowledge and skills. You will be required to demonstrate that you understand social studies concepts and are able to apply requisite skills and processes.

TEST STRUCTURE

There are 60 multiple-choice questions. The exam is composed of two booklets: a Source Booklet that contains all the sources required to answer the questions, and a question booklet that contains the questions. The sources are grouped according to theme, and each theme is generally composed of three to four sources. Some of the questions pertain to single sources within a theme, and some of the questions require you to use two or more of the sources to answer a question. Approximately 80% of this part of the exam (about 48 questions) is source-based. The remaining questions do not require sources. Instead, they rely on your knowledge of the material for Social Studies 30-1.

TEST BLUEPRINT

In order to provide a test that follows the Social Studies Program of Studies, Alberta Education has created a blueprint, or outline, for this exam. The blueprint reflects the amount of content that is outlined for each of the Related Issues outlined in the Program of Studies. There are four Related Issues, but they are not all equal in the amount of content is covered in Social Studies 30-1. In order to reflect this inequality, Alberta Education has outlined how many questions there may be on each Related Issue in the multiple-choice portion of the exam.

	Related Issue 1	Related Issue 2	Related Issue 3	Related Issue 4	Total Questions
Total Questions	4–12 Questions	20–26 Questions	20–26 Questions	4–12 Questions	60 Questions

You can see from this chart that the majority of questions will come from Related Issues 2 and 3. Keep this in mind as you study for this important exam; focus your studying on what is important to help you do your best on this exam.

CONNECTION TO THE TEXTBOOK

Before you begin to look at the rest of this study guide, it is important that you have one last piece of information related to the structure of the course as well as the exam. It is important to see how the units on the previous chart on the composition of the exam correspond to the textbook *Perspectives on Ideology* that most of you probably use. The following chart identifies the chapters that correspond to each Related Issue.

	Related Issue 1	Related Issue 2	Related Issue 3	Related Issue 4
Chapters	Introduction and Chapters 1 and 2	Chapters 3 to 8	Chapters 9 to 12	Chapters 13 and 14

You can see from this chart how the blueprint for the multiple-choice portion of the exam was developed. As you work your way through the next portions of the study guide, keep this in the back of your mind. Good luck in achieving your goals!

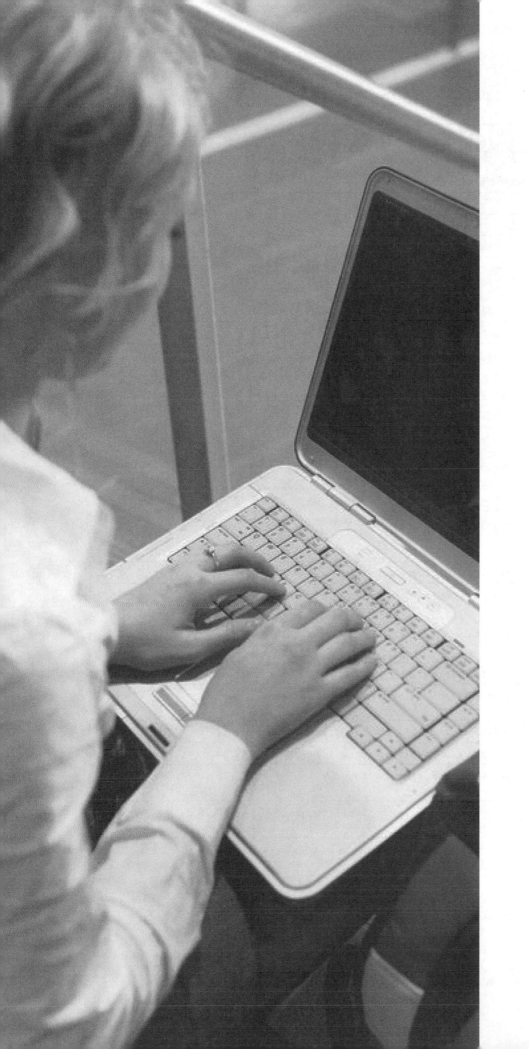

Practice Tests

PRACTICE TESTS

Table of Correlations		
Specific Outcome	**Practice Test 1**	**Practice Test 2**
By the end of this course, students will:		
12.1 *Students will explore the relationship between identity and ideology*		
12.1.3 explore factors that may influence individual and collective beliefs and values		1, 2, 3
12.1.4 examine historic and contemporary expressions of individualism and collectivism		4, 5, 6, 7
12.1.6 explore themes of ideologies	3	8, 10
12.1.7 analyze individualism as a foundation of ideology		9
12.1.8 analyze collectivism as a foundation of ideology	2	
12.1.9 analyze the dynamic between individualism and common good in contemporary societies	1	11, 12, 13
12.1.10 evaluate the extent to which personal identity should be shaped by ideologies		14, 15
12.2 *Students will assess impacts of, and reactions to, principles of liberalism*		
12.2.5 examine the relationship between the principles of liberalism and the origins of classical liberal thought	4, 5, 51, 52	16, 17, 18
12.2.6 analyze the impacts of classical liberal thought on 19th century society	6, 7, 38	39, 40
12.2.7 analyze ideologies that developed in response to classical liberalism	29, 30	19, 20
12.2.8 analyze the evolution of modern liberalism as a response to classical liberalism	8, 21, 22, 23, 24, 25, 46, 53, 54, 55, 56	
12.2.9 evaluate ideological systems that rejected principles of liberalism	49, 50, 57, 58	36, 37, 38
12.2.10 analyze how ideological conflict shaped international relations after the Second World War	47, 48	21, 22, 23
12.2.12 analyze analyze the extent to which modern liberalism is challenged by alternative thought	41, 42, 43, 44, 45, 59, 60	24, 25, 26, 27, 28, 29, 30
12.3 *Students will assess the extent to which the principles of liberalism are viable in a contemporary world*		
12.2.5 analyze the extent to which the practices of political and economic systems reflect principles of liberalism	9, 10	31, 32, 33
12.2.6 analyze the extent to which liberal democracies reflect principles of liberalism	11, 12	34, 35
12.2.7 analyze why the practices of governments may not reflect principles of liberalism	13, 14	41, 42, 43
12.2.8 evaluate the extent to which governments should promote individual and collective rights	15, 16	44, 45, 46, 47
12.2.9 evaluate the extent to which the principles of liberalism are viable in the context of contemporary issues	17, 18, 19, 20	48, 50, 51, 60

12.4	Students will assess their rights, roles, and responsibilities as citizens		
12.4.4	explore the relationship between personal and collective world views and ideology		52, 53, 54
12.4.5	explore how ideologies shape individual and collective citizenship	26, 27, 28	55, 56, 57
12.4.6	analyze perspectives on the rights, roles, and responsibilities of the individual in a democratic society (respect for law and order, dissent, civility, political participation, citizen advocacy)	31, 32, 33, 34, 35	
12.4.7	analyze perspectives on the rights, roles, and responsibilities of the individual during times of conflict (humanitarian crises, civil rights movements, antiwar movements, McCarthyism, pro-democracy movements, contemporary examples)	36, 37, 39, 40	49, 58, 59

PART A: WRITTEN

OVERVIEW

The Grade 12 Social Studies 30 final mark is composed of 50% classroom mark and 50% Diploma Examination mark. The Diploma Examination is split into two parts; Part A: Written and Part B: Multiple Choice. Each of these parts is worth 50% equally of the Diploma Examination Mark. This section of *The Key* will focus on the Part A: Written portion of the Diploma Examination.

The written portion of the Diploma Examination is composed of two assignments: a Source Analysis and a Position Paper.

In the Source Analysis you are required to interpret three sources, explain the ideological perspective for each source and discuss the links to the principles of liberalism. As well, you must identify and explain one or more of the relationships that exist among the three sources.

The Position Paper requires you to analyze a source and demonstrate an understanding of the ideological perspective reflected in the source. You are also to establish and argue a position relative to the ideological perspective presented in the source. You must support your position using evidence from your understanding and knowledge of social studies.

ASSIGNMENT 1: SOURCE ANALYSIS

DESCRIPTION OF ASSIGNMENT

You must examine and interpret three sources. To be successful structurally, you need to use paragraph form. You are to interpret each source, discuss the ideological perspectives presented, and explain the links between the principles of liberalism and each source. Lastly, you must identify and explain one or more of the relationships that exist among and between the sources. This assignment is designed to let students exhibit skills of analysis, interpretation and synthesis of a variety of sources. Answers generated will exhibit the quality of thought and communication that is expected of students in Social Studies 30-1.

This particular task will remain the same for each diploma examination administration. However, the sources will change from administration. The sources examined might include quotes, cartoons, charts, graphs, photographs, paintings or maps. Currently students have been examining three sources as part of this assignment.

ASSESSMENT CATEGORIES

There are three separate assessment categories in Assignment I. There will be a mark for the Interpretation of Sources (there will actually be three marks—one for each of the three sources—that are blended into one mark), a mark for the Identification of Relationships between each of the sources and a mark for Communication.

INTERPRETATION OF SOURCES

In the Interpretation of Sources you will be expected to interpret and explain each source as well as identify the ideological perspective presented in each source. You must also link the principles of liberalism to each source. This requires identifying the source as representing modern or classical liberalism and explaining why. To a lesser extent, you will also be looking at individualism or collectivism. You are expected to address all three sources as you are given a separate mark for each source interpretation and you could receive a "0" for any sources not interpreted. You may present this analysis in three separate paragraphs with one for each source or in a holistic fashion. Reports indicate that to be more successful and have a good chance at a fair mark you should use the individual paragraph approach in the interpretation of the sources.

IDENTIFICATION OF RELATIONSHIPS

This section will be composed of a separate paragraph where you identify the similarities and differences that exist between the three sources. You will be marked on how well you identify the relationships that exist among the sources and explain the relationships that exist among the sources. You will need to identify which two sources are similar and which one source is dissimilar. You will have to explain why you chose the two that are similar and what makes the other source dissimilar. Your success will be determined by the depth and detail that you present in your interpretation.

COMMUNICATION

Your mark for Communication is based on how well you communicate your response. Essentially this mark is for your level of vocabulary, your sentence structure and your mechanics, grammar, and organization. To do well, your vocabulary should be precise and deliberate while your sentence structure should be controlled and sophisticated. As well, your writing should show skilful control of mechanics and grammar and your writing should be judiciously organized. Please note that the mark for Communication is also determined by the length and complexity of the response. If you write a short and correct response, it does not mean that you will get an excellent mark in the area of Communication. You must show breadth and depth in your writing in order to achieve an above-satisfactory mark.

ASSIGNMENT II: POSITION PAPER

DESCRIPTION OF ASSIGNMENT

The second written assignment requires students to demonstrate the skills of analysis, evaluation, and synthesis in response to a provided written source. You will be given a written source that you must analyze, and you must demonstrate an understanding of the ideological perspective represented in the source. You will be expected to write in essay form that will reflect the quality of thought and communication expected of students in Social Studies 30-1.

This Position Paper requires you to argue a position taken in response to a question looking at the ideological perspective that is represented in the written source. You must support your position using evidence that is historical, theoretical or current events. As well, you will be expected to refer to content and vocabulary presented in the social studies course. The question itself will remain unchanged from year to year but the written source will be different in every administration.

ASSIGNMENT CATEGORIES

There are four separate assessment categories in Assignment II. There will be a separate mark for Analysis of the Source, Argument, Evidence and Communication.

ANALYSIS OF SOURCE

In this section you will required to do two things: critically analyze the source and show an understanding of the source and its relationship to an ideological perspective. In other words you will be analyzing the one source much in the same way that you analyzed the sources that you did in Assignment I. You may do the source analysis in one part of the essay or you may demonstrate this knowledge and understanding throughout your essay. A word of caution; if you want to have your work graded effectively it would be a good idea to do your analysis as a standalone part of your essay right at the beginning of your work. Spreading out your analysis throughout the essay runs the risk that it may not be graded as thoroughly as if it can be identified separately. It is important that this analysis be done or you run the risk of having your entire essay graded lower because of the lack of an analysis.

ARGUMENTATION

In the argument part of your essay you must establish a position based on the question provided. You also need to develop one or more arguments based on reason and logic. You will also have to establish a relationship between your position, your argument and the ideological perspective presented in the source. You must convincingly support a judiciously chosen and well developed argument.

EVIDENCE

The evidence portion of your essay is where you will provide the material that will effectively back up your arguments. In doing so you must make sure that your evidence is relevant and accurate and as well it should reflect depth and breadth. You may include information that you learned in the social studies course or information that you may have picked up from staying current with daily world events that might be relevant to your argument. Make sure that your evidence is as sophisticated as possible and is as accurate as possible.

COMMUNICATION

Much like in the Source Analysis portion your mark for Communication is for how well you communicate your response. Essentially this mark is for your level of vocabulary, your sentence structure and your mechanics, grammar, and organization. To do well your vocabulary should be precise and deliberate while your sentence structure should be controlled and sophisticated. As well your writing should show skilful control of mechanics and grammar and your writing should be judiciously organized. The difference with the Source Analysis is that your essay must be fluent and show a level of organization reflective of your writing. Remember that this is an essay. Please note that the mark for communication is also determined by the length and complexity of the response. If you write a short and correct response in the area of Communication it does not mean that you will get an excellent mark in this category. You must show breadth and depth in your writing in order to do above satisfactory.

SUGGESTIONS FOR SUCCESSFULLY COMPLETING THE WRITTEN RESPONSES

As you approach the two Written Response Assignments keep the following in mind in order for you to be as successful as you can.

1. Use your time effectively. Make sure that you budget your time wisely and check your exam because it will tell you approximately how much time you should allot to each assignment.

2. Read the assignment with great care. Go over the assignment carefully so that you truly understand what is required. Look over the sources so that you know the ideological perspectives that are presented.

3. Plan your work. Take the time to plan what you are going to write. Create an outline and generate ideas where you are going to take your writing. If for some reason you run out of time or the government marker does not understand what you might be trying to say then they will look at your outlines in order to give you a fair chance at a mark that reflects your marking.

4. Review your work. Before you hand your work in make sure that you review your work. This will enable you to catch mistakes that may be in your writing. This will also let you check your writing to see if it makes sense or that your arguments make sense or maybe you have left something out. Always review your writing.

Note: In the next section you will have the opportunity to look at some examples that represent different levels of writing based on the two assignments. If you wish to check out other ideas do not forget to consult what is written on the Alberta Education website with regards to Diploma Examinations. The website will provide you with the most up to date information with regards to these exams.

Following the mock-up writing assignment for a Source Analysis question there will be three exemplars that each reflects a level of writing from Satisfactory to Excellent. These exemplars are meant to provide you with an idea of what the different levels of writing could look like. They are meant to show you the depth and detail required to complete the assignment at a SS 30-1 level.

SOURCE INTERPRETATION SAMPLE ASSIGNMENT SOCIAL 30-1 RELATED ISSUE #1

Suggested Time: 30-45 minutes

Examine all sources to assist your writing of the Assignment provided.

Source I

The individual has always had to struggle to keep from being overwhelmed by the tribe. If you try it, you will be lonely often, and sometimes frightened. But no prices is too high to pay for the privilege of owning yourself.

—Friedrich Nietzsche

Source II

Source III

We are of course a nation of differences. Those differences don't make us weak. They're the source of our strength.

—Jimmy Carter

ASSIGNMENT I

What perspective(s) do each of the three sources present with regards to society's ideological pursuit of individualism and/or collectivism and what relationship(s) exists between the sources?

Examine each source. Use your knowledge and understanding of social studies and the information in the sources to write a response in paragraph form in which you:

- **Interpret** each source to identify and explain the ideological perspective(s) and their links to the principles of liberalism.

- **Identify and explain** one or more of the relationships that are reflected between the sources.

Suggestions for Writing:

- **Respond** in paragraph form organized in such a way as to effectively address both of the assigned tasks.

- **Proofread and edit** your response.

EXEMPLARS: PART A WRITTEN: SOURCE ANALYSIS

SOURCE ANALYSIS STUDENT SAMPLE I—SATISFACTORY (S)

Source 1 is saying that trying to go at it alone can be a hard, lonely struggle that will wear a person down. However it is small price to pay for being your own man. No struggle is too hard and no cost is too high to justify following others in life. Every man for himself is a very true statement. The strong survive and the weak perish. This is the attitude that brings out the best in people.

Source 2 is saying that to be an individualist in a collective society is very hard, sometimes impossible. Many people who try to live with an individualist outlook end up knocked down by the collective society's heavy punch. Being different has the downside of being left behind by other people and it's very hard to regain your feet.

Source 3 is a very individualism based quote. It is saying because every person in a nation is different, the nation is stronger because of it. Allowing each person to explore their own strengths and weaknesses allows everyone to achieve their full potential. It makes the nation more united because they have more diversity and competition among the citizens.

The first and third sources have a very individualistic based approach that is saying that going it alone is better because it allows everyone to do their best and achieve their own goals. It's sometimes hard but the end result is a happy man. Source 2 is collectivism based and it's saying that trying to be an individualist is hard on everyone and is not a viable way of life. Sources 1 and 2 use a negative view to drive home their idea while source 3 uses a positive outlook to show the benefits of individualism.

Source Analysis Student Sample II—Proficient (Pf)

Source 1 has individualistic ideals. Friedrich Nietzsche talks about how some people have to try hard to not become a part of the general community. They do this so they can keep their individuality. It also talks about how individuality can lead to loneliness or fear. Though, he says, it is always worth it to the people. He also mentions, "...owing one's self;" this idea is that there is not much government involvement and that one can support and sustain themselves by being an individual. The "fear" that he references could be that when someone is an individual, they are alone and that they will not get any help from anyone else. They feel powered by being by themselves but when they realize they are alone they only enjoy it if they are successful.

Source 2 is a cartoon by Mark Baldwin. The cartoon portrays a man in an alley with a sign that says, "CHOSE TO GO IT ALONE/PLEASE HELP;" and there is a man walking by that looks unsympathetic towards him. The man with the sign also looks very unkempt, his shoes have holes in them and his tie is ruffled. This cartoon has a collectivist point of view. The top of the sign shows that he is no longer individualistic by the sign having "please help" underneath it. The man in the alley could have given up his previous ideals to try to become a collectivist. Though this technique will probably not work it is worth it to try. The purpose of the cartoon is to show people that individualism fails when it is attempted. This man could have been trying to do anything as an individual, but now that he has realized that it's hopeless, he has just given up. This also represents the nations that try to be individualistic, they come worn out, tired and often times, weathered from poverty and inflation.

Source 3 is a quotation from Jimmy Carter. This quotation is a collectivist observation. It is about the differences within a nation. It says that the nation is made stronger from the differences, and it clearly states that they do not make the nation weaker. The reason behind the differences making them stronger could be that the ideals are of collectivist multiculturalism and all the different groups within the nation are working together to create a stronger nation. The source is most likely from someone with a pro-collectivist attitude, they would believe that collectivism creates strength within countries and nations and that everyone should help each other to make a connected group. Canada is an example of this, there are many different racial groups and the country is very strong and everyone gets along with each other very well. This says that collectivism brings us all together to help everyone be strong at the same time.

In all the sources, the errors within individualism are recognized. The first source says that if someone is individualist, they will most likely be lonely and afraid. Source 2 says that individualism leads to failure, poverty, and defeat. Source 3 identifies that individualism and multiculturalism cannot co-exist. Individualists believe in capitalism and a free market. Capitalism and a free market lead to little or no government interaction. When the government does not interact with the citizens this makes some people lonely and afraid that they have to do everything on their own. Loneliness is a large factor of failure in society, if people do not have anyone supporting them they do not want to continue what they are doing. The groups within a country also need to interact peacefully in order to keep a healthy nation. If this is not in action, the entire country fails and other countries start to care less about them.

SOURCE ANALYSIS STUDENT SAMPLE III— EXCELLENT (E)

Nietzsche in this source displays a sense of independency and qualities of individualism. He recognizes the struggles often faced when choosing the road of independence, but in doing so desires and finds pleasure in the feeling of liberation and self-satisfaction when triumph is achieved. One who matches this opinion was Thomas Hobbes. He strongly valued extreme individualism; the idea to do whatever it takes to reach the prize removing anything or anyone in the way. A great demonstration of this idea of independence is specific native tribal traditions of the transformation from boyhood to manhood. Often tradition is that when a young man reaches his early teens the difficult task of slaying an animal is expected in order for him to end his adolescence. This challenge comes with great difficulty because as a rule generally the hunting is done communally as a tribe. When the challenge is successfully achieved unaccompanied, it is then one feels the most pride and honor of accomplishment and the title of no longer a child but a man is gained. It is the inner satisfaction of independence that makes refraining from joint assistance all worth the while.

The cartoon in the second source clearly expresses failure when individualist actions are pursued. The man on the ground draws attention to those passing by. His sign shows that he recognizes how his attempt to "to at it alone" resulted unsuccessfully and is now begging for the aid of those surrounding him. He previously chose to refrain from reaching success collectively and now is feeling judgment of those around him how frown upon his disparity. Individualism values freedom and worth of one's self over the potential harmony and success of a group. Consider a basketball team. During a five on five game there is plenty of skill that must be acquired for success to be attained. But what overrides one's individual skill is the overall team unity, communication and willingness to work together. As soon as one player decides to navigate away from these principles, the overall team goal diminishes by becoming solely independent on their own skill to win the game. The rest of the play turns to shambles for that team because they are no longer unified as a whole but rather as separate individuals competing against the opposing team who display unity and discipline in working as one unit to accomplish the target set forth. When the player responsible for straying away from the team realizes the damage done to the rest, it becomes very difficult for redemption to be gained. Like this illustration the man in the picture is now facing difficulties due to lack of initial communal efforts he put forth; and is now in need of assistance from those he avoided in communing with.

In the third source Jimmy Carter proves to be a strong supporter of collectivist thinking. The collectivist society values the entire group's input and holds individuals responsible for the actions whose mindset is what everyone's doing to reach the communal goal, in comparison to for one's own selfish desires. For it makes a point to acknowledge individual's unique qualities that make up the nation as a whole. He makes it clear that if countries lacked the individual differences they acquire the result would be catastrophic simply because everyone has those differences that adds to the colorfulness of a nation. Canada is a great supporter of collective ideals. Currently in Alberta, specifically in the workforce you can see numerous races and ethnic backgrounds co-mingling to better provide variation and new ideas to entrepreneurs, in turn benefiting many consumers. Those differences collectively bring a sense of unity to the minds of the individuals involved.

Sample Student Writing and Scoring Rationales

Exemplar 1: "S"—Satisfactory

This exemplar provides an example of what could be called a basic "S" (Satisfactory) presentation in all scoring categories as laid out by Alberta Education. Each Source Analysis is adequate, straightforward, and conventional. You can see that the analysis are very basic and are generally short on detail. The links to the principles of liberalism are relevant and developed in a generalized fashion. These links are barely mentioned and as such reinforce the satisfactory nature of this paper.

The second part of this assignment is the Identification of Relationships. As with the Source Analysis this paper meets the requirement for a basis "S" presentation. It can be said that the relationships are generally and adequately identified. You can see that each of the sources is mentioned and there is an attempt to compare and contrast the sources. The explanation is generally straightforward and conventional.

Lastly there is the mark for communication. Again this paper meets the "S" requirement for this category. First of all you must understand that sometimes this mark is based on the complexity and length of the response. This is a very basic response and it is lacking in the length department with regards to completing the assignment effectively. The vocabulary is conventional and generalized and the sentence structure is controlled and straightforward. There is basic control of mechanics and grammar and the writing is adequately organized.

Exemplar 2: "Pf"—Proficient

The second exemplar shows the progression from a general "S" analysis up the next level to a general "Pf" (Proficient) level of writing. You will notice this time that the three source analyses for this paper are of a much higher level than the first exemplar. In Exemplar 2 you will notice how much more interpretation and explanation is included and how much better the links to the principles of liberalism are included. This time the interpretation and explanation is sound, specific and adept. The links to the principles of liberalism are consistent, logical and capably developed.

In the Identification of Relationship category this exemplar shows that the relationships are clearly and capably identified. The explanation is appropriate and purposeful. You will notice in this exemplar how each of the sources are compared with one another and how detailed that comparison is. There is great care taken in making sure that the comparisons of all three sources is detailed and complete. You can see how this comparison is beyond the first exemplar.

Because the ideas are more complete and sophisticated the writing naturally moves up a level in its complexity. Length naturally progresses with added details and ideas. This time the vocabulary is more appropriate and specific to the task. Sentence structure is controlled and effective in communicating the main ideas. There is capable control of mechanics and grammar and this time the writing is purposefully organized.

Exemplar 3: "E"—Excellent

The final exemplar in this section illustrates an analysis done at the "E" (Excellent) level. It is the final paper in the progression from "S" to "E". You can see that in this exemplar the writer has taken the writing to the next level in terms of analysis and detail. The Interpretation of Sources is carried out in a sophisticated, insightful and precise manner. The writing goes above and beyond in providing analysis and it is very thorough in including both current events and personal experience applications to help analyze the sources. This is a perfect example in looking at the sources. Because of the depth of the analysis it carries over to the links to the principles of liberalism and it makes this part accurate, perceptive and comprehensive.

The Identification of Relationships is excellent in this piece as well. The relationships are accurately and perceptively identified. There is great insight in how these relationships are identified. The depth of the identification of the relationships is impressive and again very detailed in looking at how the sources all fit together. All of this together makes the explanation thorough and comprehensive.

The sophistication of this response is possible partly because of the level of the communication. The vocabulary is very precise and you can see that it is deliberately chosen to communicate the ideas that it does. Going hand in hand with this is the sentence structure that is controlled and sophisticated. Finally the writing demonstrates skilful control of mechanics and grammar and it is judiciously organized. This is an example of a piece of writing that exhibits the maturity that can be achieved by the end of SS 30-1.

Source Interpretation Scoring Rationales

Scoring Criteria	Rationale	Score
Interpretation of Source I Interpretation and explanation of the source is adequate, straightforward, and conventional, demonstrating a generalized understanding of the links to liberalism.	**The student offers a straightforward interpretation of the source** ("going it alone can be a hard, lonely struggle that will wear a person down. However it is a small price to pay for being your own man.") **The rationale that** "No struggle is too hard and no cost is too high to justify following others in life." **(p. 1) is conventional and generalized.** The student asserts that individual freedoms are worth the cost, which is relevant. The idea is left generalized and not explored in depth.	S
Interpretation of Source II	The student's interpretation is conventional and straightforward ("to be an individualist in a collective society is very hard"). The explanation is adequate. The observation that individualism is difficult to practice in a collective society is relevant. It is left in general terms ("Being different has the downside of being left behind by other people").	S

Interpretation of Source III	The student offers a straightforward interpretation of the source ("because every person in a nation is different, the nation is stronger because of it.) The student's observation is relevant and generalized ("Allowing each person to explore their own strengths and weaknesses allows everyone to achieve their full potential.)	**S**
Identification of Relationships The explanation of relationship(s) is adequate and straightforward.	The student adequately identifies the relationships between the sources and liberalism, based on whether they promote individualism or collectivism **The explanation is conventional and couched in general** terms (for example, "going it alone is better because it allows everyone to do their best.")	**S**
Communication Vocabulary is conventional and generalized. Sentence structure is controlled and straightforward The writing demonstrates basic control of mechanics and grammar and is adequately organized.	The vocabulary is conventional and generalized, and makes little use of social studies terms; the paragraphs are too short to provide more than general interpretations. Grammar and structure are adequate, and errors, while present, do not significantly affect the student's argument. The student demonstrates control in writing (for example, "Allowing each person to explore their own strengths and weaknesses allows everyone to achieve their full potential.").	**S**

Scoring Criteria	Rationale	Score
Interpretation of Source I Interpretation and explanation of the source is sound, specific, and adept, demonstrating a perceptive understanding of links to liberalism.	**The student offers a sound and specific interpretation of the source** ("Friedrich Nietzsche talks about how some people have to try hard to not become a part of the general community. They do this so they can keep their individuality.") **The link to the principles of liberalism are consistent and logical** ("…this idea is that there is not much government involvement and that one can support and sustain themselves by being an individual.")	**Pf**
Interpretation of Source II	**The student provides a focussed view of the source** ("The purpose of the cartoon is to show people that individualism fails when it is attempted.") that is both sound and specific. The student links the source to the importance of community in liberal democracies, and develops this link to include nations as well as individuals.	**Pf**

Interpretation of Source III	The student interprets the source adeptly ("The reason behind the differences making them stronger could be that the ideals are of collectivist multiculturalism and all the different groups within the nation are working together to create a stronger nation.") The student's assertions are consistent with the principles of liberalism; the example of Canada is a logical extension of those assertions.	**Pf**
Identification of Relationships The explanation of relationship(s) is capable and purposeful.	**The student chooses to focus on individualism as the characteristic linking the three sources** ("In all the sources, the errors within individualism are recognized."), **clearly and capably identifying the relationships among them.** The explanation is relatively simple, but undeniably clear and purposeful.	**Pf**
Communication Vocabulary is appropriate and specific. Sentence structure is controlled and effective. **The writing demonstrates capable control of mechanics and grammar and is purposefully organized.**	Vocabulary is appropriate and specific, including such terms as "weathered", "collectivist multiculturalism", and "interaction". Sentence structure is controlled and effective, and minor errors in grammar and syntax do not detract from the analysis. The analysis is particularly well-organized. Frequent use of tentative language (for example, "could have", "most likely") weakens the prose slightly.	**Pf**

Scoring Criteria	Rationale	Score
Interpretation of Source I Interpretation and explanation of the source is sophisticated, insightful, and precise, demonstrating a perceptive understanding of links to liberalism.	**The student provides a precise and sophisticated interpretation of the source. ("He recognizes the struggles often faced when choosing the road of independence, but in doing so desires and finds pleasure in the feeling of liberation and self-satisfaction when triumph is achieved.")** The student explicitly links the quote with the principles of independence and liberty, and provides a comprehensive example to illustrate the link.	**E**

Interpretation of Source II	The student's interpretation is insightful, and takes into account the man's relationship with his wider community. ("…the man in the picture is now facing difficulties due to lack of initial communal efforts he put forth; and is now in need of assistance from those he avoided in communing with.) The student's example accurately links the source to the question of individualism vs. collectivism. The comparison to team sports is perceptive.	E
Interpretation of Source III	The student's response is sophisticated, and precisely identifies the value of individualism in achieving collective goals (The collectivist society values the entire groups input and holds individuals responsible for their actions whose mindset is what everyone's doings to reach the communal goal, in comparison to for one's own selfish desires.") The student accurately links the source with examples of harmony among individuals in a liberal democracy.	E
Identification of Relationships The explanation of relationships is perceptive and thorough.	The student clearly and accurately discusses the relationship between individualism and collectivism, weighing each source separately and coming to a distinct conclusion. The explanation is thorough and comprehensively summarizes each source and its interpretation.	E
Communication Vocabulary is precise and deliberately chosen. Sentence structure is controlled and sophisticated. The writing demonstrates skillful control of mechanics and grammar and is judiciously organized.	The student uses precise and deliberately chosen words, such as "redemption", "mindset", and "catastrophic". The student demonstrates skillful use of grammar, structure, and sentence mechanics (for example, "Source 1 demonstrates how with the right circumstances and situation individualism can result in positive internal pride and satisfaction in comparison to the second source.")	E

POSITION PAPER SAMPLE ASSIGNMENT

Analyze the following source and complete the assignment:

Following the mock-up writing assignment for a Position Paper question there will be three exemplars that each reflects a level of writing from Satisfactory to Excellent. These exemplars are meant to provide you with an idea of what the different levels of writing could look like. They are meant to show you the depth and detail required to complete the assignment at a SS 30-1 level.

SOURCE

More and more, when faced with the world of men, the only reaction is one of individualism. Man alone is an end unto himself. Everything one tries to do for the common good ends in failure.

Albert Camus

ASSIGNMENT

To what extent should we embrace the ideological perspective(s) reflected in the source?

Write an essay in which you must:

- Analyze the source and demonstrate an understanding of the ideological perspective(s) reflected in the source

- Establish and argue a position in response to the question presented

- Support your position and arguments by using evidence from your knowledge and understanding of social studies

Reminders for writing:

- Organize your essay

- Proofread your essay

EXEMPLARS: PART A WRITTEN: POSITION PAPER

POSITION PAPER STUDENT SAMPLE I—SATISFACTORY (S)

"more and more, when faced with the world of man, the only reaction is one of individualism". In this modern society there is less cooperation than mankind once had. Working together to solve problems in society is not an accepted method anymore because of the individualist outlook of modern society." Everything one tries to do for the common good ends in failure". He's saying that working together to solve problems is a recipe for failure. This source is very individualist based because of the negative shots at working together for the common good.

I disagree with the position of the source because it goes against everything our social structure and government are based on. The modern Canadian government is about serving the collective interest of the country and giving the people the opportunity to be themselves. Others will argue that an everyman for himself, strong survive weak perish ideology is a better way to go. This is untrue as some would not stop at just being the ruler of their own domain and would want to rule everyone with an iron fist. I would argue that no one person is more important than the whole country so everyone must work together in order to benefit and advance the country in a logical and practical way.

Collectivism is alive and well in modern society. Things like government services and taxes are all for the good of the entire country. We all pay income tax that allows our government to do things for us. Without these services we could not become individuals, we would all simply be a social security number in a big office in Ottawa, numbered like cattle, known only for our value to the government. Instead working together allows all of us to be ourselves and be known as people. Working together allows everyone to be different with his or hers own beliefs and values regardless of colour, background or religion. Some people say they would rather live in a more individualist based society but the general public has voted for a Government that embraces a collective ideology and it seems to be working pretty good.

People need to and do embrace collectivism in this society. With the new challenges facing the human race, now more than ever we need to work together to advance our position in life. With large obstacles such as global warming, Middle East unrest, and economy downturn looming on the horizon there is strength in numbers and we will need all the strength we can get. If it weren't for collectivism the human race would have been wiped out all ready and we will need to continue to support each other in order to survive the future.

POSITION PAPER STUDENT SAMPLE II—PROFICIENT (PF)

Even though I don't fully agree with Camus' opinion, I do believe that some of it is somewhat true and accurate. However, his perspective, in my opinion, is merely over the top. Not everything that one tries to do for the common good ends in failure, sometimes it does actually help the situation. Even if it doesn't, it's better to try to help than stand back and watch, doing nothing at all. I do agree that by being alone, in the end it'll ruin you.

For example, a sense of collectivism would have come in handy when Germany was taking over and not many other countries stepped up to help those in need. Several countries were ruined and destroyed, and it could have been prevented if more countries had joined together and attempted to help. How, we see countries fighting wars for the peace and security of other countries, like in Afghanistan. It shows how collectivism can make more of a change than just one group or person.

In conclusion, the statement said by Albert Camus isn't necessarily accurate for our times. In the early 1900's and until the end of World War II it would have been most likely more accurate, but now, as a collective society, we have more power, we can help more and have more of a chance of success than we would have as individualists. I believe there's a better chance of making an actual difference when in a collective than there is as an individual, unlike Camus states. If we all work together, we can make a difference.

POSITION PAPER STUDENT SAMPLE III– EXCELLENT (E)

Collectivism reinforces the idea that makes some sort of group rather than the individual, the fundamental unit of political, social, and economic concern. Collectivists insist that the claims of groups, associations, or government must normally overtake the claims of individuals. On the contrary individualists' are of ethical independence that a human being should think and judge independently, respecting nothing more than the dominion of his or her mind; hence, it is ultimately connected with the concept of self-rule. As an ethical-political concept, individualism upholds the power of individual rights. Camus suggests that collectivism ultimately ends in failure. Embracing collectivism is the only way to drive a country to success. Individually it is the people's responsibility to bring individuals together for the greater good of the nation through collective thinking.

Performing together for the greater good of a community for thousands of years has proven to be a majorly successful way of acting, thinking, and communicating. To this day and for many years Libya has suffered great corruption as a country under a totalitarian dictatorship. One man and his family singlehandedly run and controlled the nation with great force, solely for their own personal benefit; which in turn has taken a drastic toll on the nation's stability and wellbeing. Currently the people of the country are beginning to take a collectivist approach at addressing the issues of the poverty stricken land that has been puppeteered by their dictator, the one responsible for their disparity. The people of Libya have together as one stood up and revolted against the one who pleasures in controlling their strings. Against the one who has failed those he leads due to his need for individual power and in doing so failed himself and his family. It is enormous calamity in the land at this time and day and impressive news to the rest of the viewing world. Outside countries are seeing the Libyan people join in unison to fight for what should be their rights. The impact they have made is tremendous, but this would never have been even close to possible if lone civilians took the attack unaccompanied with the message of demands coming from only one body. Attention for aid and support of these matters are now drawn by the eyes of all nations, all thanks to the coming together of the civilians as one.

To understand the collectivist ideology you must recognize the success available that comes when one has the privilege to belong to a certain group, it may be through nearly anything. A great example is the unity required in sports teams in order to succeed. Whether it be doubles in tennis on the court, or the fifty four rugged football players competing on field. They all strive to reach the same goal. That goal is to claim the title of the ultimate champion together as a team. Take American football for example. The reason for the vast numbers of players on a team is because it takes multiple positions to be filled during the play in order to receive, recover and score profitably. Thomas Hobbes would have been fond of this sport because football requires one player, the quarterback to call the shots on the team. It is he who every other single offensive player listens for to know what play to execute; to know who to protect and to know who to take out. It is with the quarterbacks' wisdom in leading the men that allows opportunity for a touchdown. If any other individual tries to override the quarter back say of authority, they in turn send mixed messages to the rest. It is then that disaster becomes in order. Without proper communal execution from the rest of the players then the playmaker is made vulnerable and the opposition will attack the opportunity to regain possession, leaving the rest scattered and in defense. Without the entire team on the same page failure is expected.

Hobbes was in favour of a monarchy mainly because he believed there should be one supreme authority. He could tolerate parliament alone, but not a system in which power of the government is shared. This way it would be the community benefiting from their together efforts. This in a way could potentially benefit a community by having them on the same page, working together. But as soon as that one individual leading does something wrong in the eyes of the rest they bind together to overthrow that one man's individualist thinking. Like in football, this example demonstrates how even when individualist thinking is attempted and considered that collective thinking has to take over when faults are made.

Rousseau believed people are inherently good and have been corrupted by civilization and society. He was a supporter of democracy which supports and suggests making decisions as a nation. Residences of Canada have experienced firsthand the blessing of a democratic government. Canadian citizens have the privilege of having a say in decisions that their country makes by voting for a political leader and party to guide the country in the way of the voters. These parties act as representatives of people who collectively believe in the same morals and opinion on conflicting matters. This way of government allows for individuals with the same opinion on matters to be heard. If one were to compare a collectivist type government to an individualistic monarch, he would realize that a democracy has numerous upsides in comparison. A monarchy is ruled by one. No one is entitles to, without potential extreme consequences a say of how people in the nation are feeling, what they want or are even concerned with. The one leader in power calls all the shots according specifically their opinion on the matter. And more often than not does damage to the nation that the civilians suffer from, resulting in revolt; just like the ruckus happening in Libya to this day.

Throughout history we have had opportunity to observe firsthand results of people's failure to succeed in selfish attempts to excel individually. Results of achievement or letdown of one's personal goals when reached is kept confined, singlehandedly celebrated and the weight of the loss remains all on one individuals shoulders. There is no doubt that the groups who work communally together for the greater good have too stumbled and attained failure. But in doing so together had opportunity to learn from those faults and grow together to progress, improve and step forward as a whole learning from the past. Contrary to individualists, collectivist ways when success is accomplished allows for a greater overall achievement and a step forward. Camus was absolutely right when he points out "man alone is an end unto himself". He makes it very clear that those going at it unaided are only asking for a struggle. The only way to avoid the controversy is to charge with numbers. One easily can see this through these proofs of history, government, communal affairs and current worldly events. And one should now know, a man wins battles, but an army wins wars.

SAMPLE STUDENT WRITING AND SCORING RATIONALES

EXEMPLAR 1: "S"—SATISFACTORY

This exemplar provides an example of what could be called a basic "S" (Satisfactory) presentation in all scoring categories as laid out by Alberta Education. The first part of the assignment requires you to do a source analysis much like you had to do in the first part of the Written Assignment. In Exemplar 1 the analysis of the source is straightforward and conventional. You will notice that the analysis of the source takes place right at the start of the paper and then the student goes on with the rest of the paper. In order to have your Source Analysis considered by the marker at central marking it is advisable to do it right at the start of the paper. This way you will know that your analysis will be marked. If you spread your analysis out through your paper you run the risk of part of your analysis being missed by the marker. In this exemplar you will notice that the understanding of the source and its relationship to an ideological perspective is adequately demonstrated.

The second mark awarded in the Position Paper deals with Argumentation. In this paper you will see that the position established is generally supported by appropriately chosen and developed arguments. In other words the argument in the paper is easy to understand but it is straightforward and pretty conventional in demonstrating an adequate understanding of the assignment. Lastly the relationship between the position taken, argumentation, and the ideological perspective presented in the source is generally developed.

The third mark awarded in the Position Paper deals with Evidence. In other words this section deals with the evidence that is provided to support the argument in the paper. The evidence is marked on how relevant and accurate it is and its depth and breadth in the paper. Exemplar 1 is satisfactory in this area because the evidence is conventional and straightforward. In this exemplar there is an amount of evidence listed and it is relevant to some degree but there is no depth provided in the analysis of this information. Therefore this becomes a generalized and basic discussion that reveals an acceptable understanding of social studies knowledge and its application to the assignment.

The fourth mark awarded is in the area of communication. This time Communication refers to fluency and essay organization as well as syntax, mechanics and grammar. Lastly is the use of vocabulary and social studies terminology. As was indicated in the section on Source Analysis the mark for Communication can be affected by the proportion of error in relation to the complexity and length of the response to the assigned task. In other words simple writing with no mistakes does not necessarily generate an excellent mark in Communication. In the case of Exemplar 1 the writing is straightforward and functionally organized. The control of syntax, mechanics and grammar is adequate. The vocabulary is conventional and generalized. Overall the communication is generally clear.

Exemplar 2: "Pf"—Proficient:

The second exemplar shows the progression from a general "S" analysis up the next level to a general "Pf" (Proficient) level of writing. The first thing you will notice with this exemplar is that the analysis is to the point and it incorporates an added dimension by reference to the author. Now while this may not be possible all the time, in this situation this knowledge adds to the source analysis. This exemplar also shows that it is possible to refer back to the source during the writing to help establish and explain the arguments. This makes the critical analysis of the source sound and adept. As well the understanding of the source and its relationship to an ideological perspective is capably demonstrated.

The argumentation in this exemplar is one step up from the first one because this time the author's position is established persuasively and supported by purposely chosen and developed arguments. You can see that this is a stronger voice in this paper and a clearer understanding of what the author wants to communicate is presented. The argumentation is logical and capably developed, demonstrating a sound understanding of the assignment. Throughout this paper the relationship between the argument and the ideological perspective presented is clearly developed.

The evidence to support this argument is specific and purposeful. While a few more examples or details would elevate this paper even more the evidence provided does enhance the argument. The evidence reveals a solid understanding of social studies knowledge as well as relevant knowledge that is beyond the program of studies and as was mentioned was well chosen to back up the argument.

The communication in this paper is very proficient in how it communicates the arguments and ideas presented. The writing is clear and purposefully organized and this can be seen through the transition between and among the paragraphs. This organization helps exhibit the capable control of syntax, mechanics and grammar in this paper. In this paper the vocabulary appropriate to the assignment and this time a little more specific and this help enhance the argument in this paper. Any minor errors in language do not impede communication.

Exemplar 3: "E"—Excellent:

The last of these exemplars shows the end in the progression from satisfactory to excellent. This paper shows the upper end in writing of the position paper. The analysis here is on a higher level in that its analysis is all related to a discussion on collectivism and individualism. This is a very direct and high level approach to this. This makes the analysis insightful and sophisticated. In the end this shows that the understanding of the source and its relationship to an ideological perspective is very comprehensive.

As you read this paper you will notice that the position established at the start of this paper is convincingly supported by judiciously chosen and developed arguments. The arguments in this paper are consistent and compelling and all of this demonstrates an insightful understanding of the assignment. The relationship between the position taken, the arguments and the ideological perspective presented in the source is perceptively developed. The sophistication in the arguments shows how you can write at the upper level if you concentrate on blending the source with your arguments on the topic. If you provide passion and insight in your arguments you will be able to score above average in your writing.

An argument can only be strong if there is accurate and sophisticated evidence to back it up and this paper is a good example of this. The evidence is very relevant and accurate in fact it is sophisticated and deliberately chosen. The evidence is so perceptive and supports the arguments in a mature manner. You will find evidence in this paper that refers to thinkers that are studied in SS 30-1 as well as current events and events from the world of the author. The relative absence of error in the selection of evidence is impressive. The evidence used in this paper provides for a thorough and comprehensive discussion. All of this together reveals an insightful understanding of social studies knowledge and its application to the assignment.

In order to present these arguments and evidence effectively the writing in this piece is fluent, skilfully structured and judiciously organized. Considering the length of this piece there is sophisticated control of syntax, mechanics and grammar. While there might be a couple of issues with some of the vocabulary this is where there was a risk taken by the author. The length and sophistication of the piece allows for risk and in the end the vocabulary is precise and deliberately chosen. The relative absence of error is impressive. All in all, this piece is a thorough example of an "E" that illustrates what can be achieved in SS 30-1.

It is hoped that with the preceding two sets of exemplars that you have been able to see the progression between an "S" and an "E" and that you will be able to make some observations that will improve your writing in SS 30-1 and on the Diploma Examinations. Always think about your writing before, during and after the writing process and ask yourself, "What can I do to make it better?"

POSITION PAPER SCORING RATIONALES

Scoring Criteria	Rationale	Score
Analysis of Source The analysis of the source is conventional and straightforward; a generalized understanding of the ideological perspective(s) is demonstrated.	**The critical analysis of the source is straightforward and conventional:** "He's saying that working together to solve problems is a recipe for failure. This source is very individualist based because of the negative shots at working together for the common good." The student adequately demonstrates an understanding of the source and its relationship to an ideological perspective. The student asserts a tacit but logical link between extreme individualism and various negative consequences (social Darwinism, Hobbes's concept of the war of all against all, etc.).	S

Argumentation	The student's position is clear and appropriately argued. ("I would argue that no one person is more important than the whole country so everyone must work together in order to benefit and advance the country in a logical and practical way.") The student uses Canadian culture and politics to illustrate and develop the argument. The argumentation is straightforward and conventional, demonstrating an adequate understanding of the assignment. In broad terms, the student refutes the source by emphasizing the benefits of a collective mindset. The relationship between the source and the argument is generally developed, with the source taken as an exemplar of individualism and Canada as an exemplar of collectivism.	**S**
The position established is generally supported by appropriately chosen and developed argument(s) The argumentation is straightforward and conventional, demonstrating an adequate understanding of the assignment. The relationship between the position taken, argumentation, and the ideological perspective presented in the source is generally developed.		
Evidence Evidence is conventional and straightforward. The evidence may contain minor errors and a mixture of relevant and extraneous information. A generalized and basic discussion reveals an acceptable understanding of social studies knowledge and its application to the assignment.	Evidence is conventional, relevant and straightforward. For example, the student provides a list of "monumental events" that have brought Canadians together, and cites global warming and other current crises as obstacles to be overcome. The student displays an acceptable understanding of social studies knowledge, and provides a basic discussion of collectivism and individualism, and their general implication in contemporary society.	**S**
Communication The writing is straightforward and functionally organized. Control of syntax, mechanics, and grammar is adequate. Vocabulary is conventional and generalized. There may be occasional lapses in control and minor errors; however, the communication remains generally clear.	The writing is straightforward and functionally organized. For example, "Working together allows everyone to be different with his or hers own beliefs and values regardless of colour, back ground or religion." Vocabulary is conventional, and minor errors do not obscure communication; for example, "Some people say they would rather live in a more individualist based society but the general public has voted for a Government that embraces a collective ideology and it seems to be working pretty good."	**S**
Scoring Criteria	**Rationale**	**Score**

Analysis of Source The analysis of the source is capable and adept; a sound understanding of the ideological perspective(s) is demonstrated.	The student begins with a sound analysis of the source, studying each sentence as well as the whole paragraph. It is clear that the student understands the source, and provides ample context for it. ("He was born in time for World War 1, and he lived through the Great Depression and World War 2 as well.")	**Pf**
Argumentation The position established is persuasively supported by purposefully chosen and developed argument(s). The argumentation is logical and capably developed, demonstrating a sound understanding of the assignment. The relationship between the position taken, argumentation, and the ideological perspective presented in the source is clearly developed.	The student persuasively argues that Camus's statement goes too far, and that his view was coloured by the global crises of the early 20th century; the argument is carefully developed and focused. ("For example, a sense of collectivism would have come in handy when Germany was taking over and not many countries stepped up to help those in need.") This shows that the student understands the source and its historical/political context. The student does a good job of referring the argument to both the source and its ideological perspective throughout the paper.	**Pf**
Evidence Evidence is specific and purposeful. Evidence may contain some minor errors. A capable and adept discussion of evidence reveals a solid understanding of social studies knowledge and its application to the assignment.	As mentioned above, the student specifically selects evidence from the time period in which Camus lived, and occasionally relates it to the contemporary world. The student demonstrates a solid grasp of social studies concepts and how they apply to the assignment. For example, the student adeptly compares the failure of appeasement in the interwar period to the use of military to enforce peace and security in Afghanistan.	**Pf**
Communication The writing is clear and purposefully organized. Control of syntax, mechanics, and grammar is capable. Vocabulary is appropriate and specific. Minor errors in language do not impede communication.	The writing is clear and purposefully organized. The writer has capable control of syntax, mechanics, and grammar. For example, "However, his perspective, in my opinion, is merely over the top." Vocabulary is appropriate and specific. For example, "Growing up with destruction around him would have showed him that obviously the help that others are giving isn't helping at all and that there is no point because all the work they put into giving assistance ends up going to waste." Minor errors in language do not impede communication.	**Pf**

Scoring Criteria	Rationale	Score
Analysis of Source The analysis of the source is insightful and sophisticated; a comprehensive understanding of the ideological perspective(s) is demonstrated.	**The critical analysis of the source is insightful and sophisticated:** "…individualists' are of ethical independence, that a human being should think and judge independently, respecting nothing more than the dominion of his or her mind; hence, it is ultimately connected with the concept of self-rule. As an ethical-political concept, individualism upholds the power of individual rights." The understanding of the source and its relationship to an ideological perspective is comprehensively demonstrated throughout the paper as an exemplar of individualism; it is linked to examples as diverse as Libya and American football.	**E**
Argumentation **The position established is convincingly supported by judiciously chosen and developed argument(s).** The argumentation is consistent and compelling, demonstrating an insightful understanding of the assignment. The relationship between the position taken, argumentation, and the ideological perspective presented in the source is perceptively developed.	**The student's position—that** "Embracing collectivism is the only way to drive a country to success"**—is convincingly supported by judiciously chosen and developed arguments. For example,** "Canadian citizens have the privilege of having a say in decisions that their country makes by voting for a political leader and party to guide the country in the way of the voters. These parties act as representatives of people who collectively believe in the same morals and opinion on conflicting matters. This way of government allows for individuals with the same opinion on matters to be heard." The student's arguments are compelling and insightful. For example, the student notes that while having a sole, identifiable leader often makes sense, that leader is still ultimately answerable to the will of the collective, even if unofficially (e.g., the recent Libyan revolution).	**E**

Evidence Evidence is sophisticated and deliberately chosen. The relative absence of error is impressive. **A thorough and comprehensive discussion of evidence reveals an insightful understanding of social studies knowledge and its application to the assignment.**	**Evidence is sophisticated and deliberately chosen. For example,** "Hobbes was in favour of a monarchy mainly because he believed there should be one supreme authority. He could tolerate parliament alone, but not a system in which power of the government is shared." The relative absence of error is impressive. There are only extremely minor issues; for example, the student does not name Muammar Gaddafi. However, the lack does not in any way harm the student's argument. The student displays an insightful understanding of social studies, correctly describing the different social contract theories of Thomas Hobbes and Jean-Jacques Rousseau. The prediction that Hobbes would be a football fan is particularly clever.	**E**
Communication The writing is fluent, skillfully structured, and judiciously organized. Control of syntax, mechanics, and grammar is sophisticated. Vocabulary is precise and deliberately chosen. **The relative absence of error is impressive.**	**The writing is fluent, skillfully structured, and judiciously organized. For example,** "Attention for aid and support of these matters are now drawn by the eyes of all nations, all thanks to the coming together of the civilians as one." Vocabulary is precise and deliberately chosen, with the student using words such as "ultimately", "totalitarian", and "communal".	**E**

PRACTICE TEST 1

Use the following source to answer the next three questions.

1. Which of the given headlines **best** illustrates the principle of the *rule of law*?

   A. *The Daily*

   B. *The Times*

   C. *The Herald*

   D. *The Express*

2. The headline in *The Herald* **best** illustrates the principle of the freedom of

   A. *speech*

   B. *religion*

   C. *thought*

   D. *assembly*

3. The given headlines **most likely** occur in a

   A. communist state

   B. feudal monarchy

   C. totalitarian nation

   D. liberal democracy

Use the following source to answer the next two questions.

Position I

Key industries should always be in the hands of the government. That way, important utilities, such as water, gas, and electricity, are insulated from market forces. It is essential for the government to control these key industries, especially in times of crisis, to ensure that citizens and businesses always have the resources they need to keep going.

Position II

All industries, key or not, should be free from government interference. Competition between suppliers means lower costs for citizens and businesses. Also, industries are run much more efficiently than government bureaucracies.

---

4. Which of the following individuals would **most likely** support the ideas in Position I?

    A. Karl Marx

    B. John Locke

    C. Adam Smith

    D. Thomas Hobbes

5. Which of the following types of ideology best represent Position II?

    A. Collectivist

    B. Communist

    C. Modern Liberal

    D. Classical Liberal

Use the following source to answer the next two questions.

Should the Canadian government be supporting Aboriginal self-government?

Speaker I

I don't think so, for a couple of reasons. First of all, Canadian citizens know that a liberal democracy is the best form of government, so a return to the tribal system of government would be a step backward. Secondly, I do not think that Aboriginal leaders would be able to address all the problems plaguing their communities—the Canadian government is far better equipped to do so.

Speaker II

Perhaps, but this is a decision best left up to the Canadian people as a whole. Let's let the citizens decide, rather than some government department. I think we should hold a nation-wide vote on this issue, and if it ends up in favour of Aboriginal self-government, then let's make it happen.

Speaker III

Absolutely. Frankly, I do not think it is the business of most Canadian citizens, since they do not fully understand the issue or what it is like to be an Aboriginal person in Canada. Enough with all this uninformed debate—if Canada's Aboriginal peoples want to govern themselves, then they should.

---

6. According to John Stuart Mill, Speaker I's viewpoint is an example of

   A. social tyranny

   B. free and open debate

   C. essential civil liberties

   D. tyranny of the majority

7. Speaker II is referring to the use of

   A. an initiative

   B. a recall vote

   C. a referendum

   D. a non-confidence vote

8. The ideas presented by Speaker III have been detailed in which of the following reports?

   A. White Paper - 1968

   B. Red Paper - 1970

   C. Canadian Constitution - 1982

   D. Commission on Aboriginal Peoples – 1996

Use the following source to answer the next two questions.

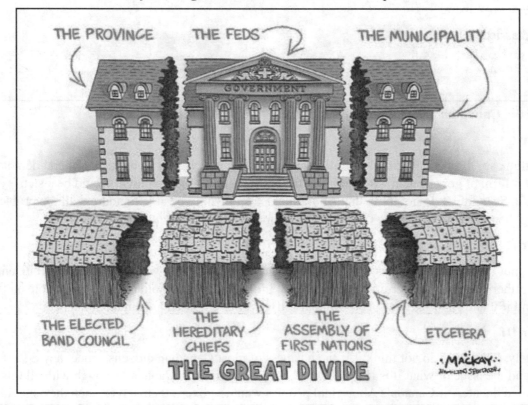

9. According to the cartoon, First Nations' issues are

  A. easy to resolve

  B. difficult to resolve

  C. the responsibility of the Federal Government

  D. the responsibility of the First Nations Peoples

10. Taken together with the source for questions 6 to 8, it would appear that the speakers mistakenly believe that Aboriginal Peoples are

  A. poor

  B. unified

  C. fractured

  D. disaffected

Use the following source to answer the next three questions.

What is the primary societal role of the government?

Speaker I

Really, the government should not have a major role in society; people can make decisions for themselves. The most important thing that the government can do is to allow citizens to work for themselves—to save money and spend it on the things they want and need. In today's society, the more wealth you have, the freer you are.

Speaker II

It's sad to say, but I think that we need the government in order to protect us from one another. I am not saying that all people are bad, but without the protection of the government, people would be stealing, fighting, and doing whatever it took to survive. The government provides us with laws, and punishes those who break them. It makes sense for people to give up their rights in order to ensure their safety.

Speaker III

In order for society to thrive, people need stability. The government can provide this not only by ensuring the safety of the citizens, but by establishing a stable social framework for society to build itself around. This leaves people free to live without undue interference from their fellow citizens.

Speaker IV

The government should be more or less indistinguishable from society. All government decisions, such as new laws, should be the decisions of the people. Only they have the right to decide what is best for them. The government, then, is a tool that the citizenry uses to carry out its collective will.

---

11. Each of the speaker's statements are based on a
    A. democratic theory
    B. social contract theory
    C. modern liberal philosophy
    D. classical liberal philosophy

12. Which two speakers share somewhat the same point of view?
    A. Speakers I and II
    B. Speakers II and III
    C. Speakers II and IV
    D. Speakers I and III

13. Speaker IV's statement is consistent with the ideas of
    A. Edmund Burke
    B. Thomas Hobbes
    C. Baron de Montesquieu
    D. Jean-Jacques Rousseau

Use the following source to answer the next two questions.

Sweat rolled down Tom's face as he shovelled coal into the mouth of the furnace. He took care not to accidentally brush against the scorching metal grate as he worked; he had a half-healed burn on his left arm as a reminder to be careful. His coal pile was getting low, so he signalled to one of the boys to bring another load. When the lad tipped the coal out onto the floor, a great cloud of coal dust billowed up, making Tom cough.

"Someone ought to clean this place up," thought Tom as he walked down the street where he lived. The ramshackle buildings on either side looked ready to fall onto the road at any moment, and Tom knew that they were packed to bursting with people like him. And the smell…
well, on a hot day, the smell rising from the gutters would sicken a rat. Tom laughed bitterly to himself. It would take a flood of biblical proportions to clean this place.

14. This source relates to the rise of
    A. socialism
    B. communism
    C. mercantilism
    D. industrialism

15. Faced with the working conditions described in source, labourers responded by

    A. forming political parties

    B. organizing labour unions

    C. moving away from cities

    D. returning to cottage industries

Use the following source to answer the next four questions.

Feature I Both the Nazis in Germany and the Communists in Russia	**Feature II** Nazis in Germany
Feature III Communists in Russia	**Feature IV** Neither the Nazis in Germany nor the Communists in Russia

16. Which group in the source replaced an unpopular government?

    A. Feature I

    B. Feature II

    C. Feature III

    D. Feature IV

17. Which group in the source seized power through a popular revolution?

    A. Feature I

    B. Feature II

    C. Feature III

    D. Feature IV

18. Which group in the source provided for the welfare of all of their citizens?

    A. Feature I

    B. Feature II

    C. Feature III

    D. Feature IV

19. Which group in the source employed a secret police force?

    A. Feature I

    B. Feature II

    C. Feature III

    D. Feature IV

Use the following source to answer the next question.

> Alejandra left the voting station with a sense of pride. She knew where each candidate stood on the issues, and she had voted for the one she felt would best represent her in parliament. Tonight, she would watch the election results on TV.

20. In the source Alejandra is participating in a

   A. direct democracy

   B. liberal democracy

   C. classical democracy

   D. representative democracy

Use the following sources to answer the next five questions.

Source I

"From Stettin in the Baltic to Trieste in the Adriatic, an iron curtain has descended across the Continent. Behind that line lie all the capitals of the ancient states of Central and Eastern Europe."

—Sir Winston Churchill

Source II

"But when internal and external forces that are hostile to Socialism try to turn the development of some Socialist country towards the restoration of a capitalist regime, when Socialism as a whole is threatened, it becomes not only the problem of the people of the country concerned, but a common problem and concern of all Socialist countries."

—former general secretary of the Soviet Union Leonid Brezhnev

Source III

"There is one sign the Soviets can make that would be unmistakable, that would advance dramatically the cause of freedom and peace. General Secretary Gorbachev, if you seek peace, if you seek prosperity for the Soviet Union and Eastern Europe, if you seek liberalization: Come here to this gate! Mr. Gorbachev, open this gate! Mr. Gorbachev, tear down this wall!"

—former president Ronald Reagan

21. In Source I, Sir Winston Churchill is **most likely** referring to the

   A. signing of the Warsaw Pact

   B. Soviet invasion of Hungary

   C. construction of the Berlin Wall

   D. spread of communism in Europe

22. Which of the following statements **best** describes what former general secretary Brezhnev is implying in Source II?

   A. Communist nations should join together in mutual defence pacts

   B. Communist nations should protect one another from capitalist nations

   C. Communist regimes should attempt to spread their ideology to neighbouring countries

   D. Communist regimes should interfere to prevent a Communist nation from becoming capitalist

23. What is former president Reagan asking for in Source III?

   A. Freedom of speech in Warsaw Pact nations

   B. Free market practices in Warsaw Pact nations

   C. Free movements to and from Warsaw Pact nations

   D. Freedom to hold free elections in Warsaw Pact nations

24. Which of the following topics **best** describes the link between the three sources?

   A. The spread of capitalism in Europe

   B. The rise and fall of the Soviet Union

   C. The Soviet Union's sphere of influence

   D. The conflict between the East and West in Europe

25. The three sources were stated during a time known as the

   A. Cold War

   B. Korean War

   C. First Gulf War

   D. Second World War

Use the following source to answer the next three questions.

What is the primary role of government?

Speaker I

The government's job is to make sure that the country runs smoothly and efficiently. I have no use for a government that spends all its time debating instead of doing. Who needs the uninformed opinions of the masses? The government sees what needs to be done and can take steps to make it happen properly and on time.

Speaker II

The government should make sure that every citizen has what he or she needs. The government is in the best position to know what goods need to be made and to distribute those goods where they are needed. I see the government as a middleman who gathers all the goods together and then distributes them fairly among the population.

Speaker III

The government exists to carry out the will of the nation's citizens. The best government is one that serves the people, rather than the other way around. It protects citizens' rights and does not interfere where it is not needed.

---

26. What type of government would Speaker I **most likely** support?
    A. Socialist
    B. Totalitarian
    C. Communist
    D. Democratic

27. Speakers II and III would **most likely** agree that the government should ensure the
    A. rights of the citizens
    B. welfare of the citizens
    C. freedoms of the citizens
    D. economic equality of the citizens

28. Which of the following initiatives would Speaker III be **most likely** to support?
    A. Higher corporate taxes
    B. The nationalization of the oil industry
    C. Increased trade with developing economies
    D. New tariffs to protect domestic industries from competition

Use the following source to answer the next two questions.

Perceived Government Responsibilities Per Age Group

Government Responsibility	18–30 % Should Be	31–40 % Should Be	41+ % Should Be
Laws to protect the environment	93.8	89.8	94.1
Provide decent housing	81.0	78.2	85.8
Control prices	75.6	70.5	69.1
Help industry grow	61.8	84.0	75.6
Provide jobs for everyone	52.6	38.0	35.0

Note: N = 1068

Question: To what extent should each of the following be a responsibility of the government?

Source: International Social Survey Programme, 2006—Work and the Role of Government data set

29. Which of the following individuals would most likely support the answers given in the first response on the chart?

   A. Adam Smith

   B. John Locke

   C. Thomas Hobbes

   D. Baron de Montesquieu

30. For which of the following essay topics would the information in the chart be most appropriately used?

   A. What is the role of Canadians and their government?

   B. How should Canadians be involved with their government?

   C. How should older Canadians view the economy and their government?

   D. What is the course of young Canadians' involvement with their government?

Use the following source to answer the next three questions.

We now recognize that it was wrong to separate children from rich and vibrant cultures and traditions that it created a void in many lives and communities, and we apologize for having done this.

We now recognize that in separating children from their families, we undermined the ability of many to adequately parent their own children and sowed the seeds for generations to follow, and we apologize for having done this.

We now recognize that, far too often, these institutions gave rise to abuse or neglect and were inadequately controlled, and we apologize for failing to protect you.

—Prime Minister Stephen Harper, June 11, 2008

31. The Canadian government created the residential school system in order to

    A. provide free education for aboriginal children

    B. teach aboriginal children about European culture

    C. assimilate aboriginal children into European culture

    D. ensure that aboriginal children learned about their native culture

32. Which of the following legacies was **not** created by the residential school system?

    A. Aboriginal culture and traditions have largely been eliminated in Canada.

    B. Residential schools undermined the parenting skills of those who attended.

    C. Those that went to residential schools were traumatized by their experiences.

    D. Aboriginal communities were damaged by the removal of children from their families.

33. Which of the following government actions was similar to the one reflected in the source?

    A. Prime Minister Trudeau apologizing for the arrests made during the October Crisis

    B. Prime Minister Martin apologizing for the arrests made during the September 11 Crisis

    C. Prime Minister Chretien apologizing for the internment of Ukrainian Canadians during the First World War.

    D. Prime Minister Mulroney apologizing for the internment of Japanese Canadians during the Second World War.

Use the following source to answer the next two questions.

34. The message in the cartoon is that even though there was an apology from the Federal Government with regards to Residential Schools

A. First Nations' Peoples were really to blame

B. the situation still plagues First Nations' Peoples

C. the apology to First Nations' Peoples was insincere

D. the Canadian government still patronizes First Nations' Peoples

35. According to the cartoon the government of Canada believes that

A. Aboriginals are content with the solution

B. a situation like this will never happen again

C. they will work with First Nations' Peoples as equals in the future

D. an apology is all that is needed to solve the Residential School situation

Use the following source to answer the next three questions.

The Daily
Supreme Court judge calls for fine for racists

The Times
War criminal denied entry into Canada

THE HERALD
"All signs must be in French," says Quebec premier

THE EXPRESS
Bird flu fears promt Canada to suspend all poultry imports

36. Which headline is **least likely** to occur in Canada?

A. *The Daily*

B. *The Times*

C. *The Herald*

D. *The Express*

37. Quebec could pass a law for all signs to be in French because

A. Quebec has its own Charter of Rights and Freedoms

B. language rights are not guaranteed in the Constitution

C. Quebec could employ the notwithstanding clause in the Contstitution

D. language laws are a provincial matter according to the Charter of Rights and Freedoms

38. Which of the following Government Acts makes the actions in *The Express* headline possible?

A. Emergencies Act

B. War Measures Act

C. Anti-Terrorism Act

D. PATRIOT Act

Use the following source to answer the next two questions.

> Canada's Liberal government is rushing to enact an "anti-terrorism" bill that breaks with key tenets of British-Canadian jurisprudence – tenets historically –developed in the struggle against arbitrary and unfettered executive power.
>
> Bill C-36 establishes a new order of "terrorist" crimes for which the state will have special investigative and prosecutorial powers. These include preventive detention – i.e. the right to incarcerate people on the mere suspicion they may be about to commit a crime; a new police power to compel testimony from anyone they believe has information pertinent to a terrorism investigation; closed trials; and a right of the prosecution, with a judge's approval, to deny an accused and his counsel full knowledge of the evidence against him.
>
> The definition of terrorism around which the legislation is constructed is so broad that it could be used to prosecute trade unionists involved in an illegal strike or those engaged in civil disobedience.
>
> Bill C-36 also greatly increases police powers of surveillance, while dramatically increasing the government's prerogative to suppress information about its activities.

39. The writer's view in the source is that Canadian Government action after September 2001 is
    A. going too far in dealing with the issue of terrorism
    B. weakening laws in dealing with the issue of terrorism
    C. reinforcing laws in dealing with the issue of terrorism
    D. not going far enough in dealing with the issue terrorism

40. Which point of view does the speaker **most likely** represent?
    A. Liberal
    B. Socialist
    C. Progressivist
    D. Conservative

Use the following source to answer the next three questions.

In which area should the government focus its spending?

Speaker I

The environment is by far the most important area. We are already seeing climate change, and unless we take action now, we are setting ourselves up for major problems down the road. Sure, there will be some financial impact now, but we will be far better off in the long term.

Speaker II

The military badly needs investment. We need to stop relying on the American military and pay more attention to our own. Not only is it our duty as a sovereign nation, it will make us more effective for peacekeeping missions. These men and women are putting their lives on the line; shouldn't we be doing our part to help them?

Speaker III

If we want to ensure a prosperous future for Canadians, let's focus on education. That is an investment with widespread benefits, not only for individual citizens, but for society as a whole. People with a solid education get better jobs, have a better income, and enjoy a higher quality of life—the statistics prove it.

Speaker IV

In my opinion, the real measure of a society is how well it takes care of its citizens. In times of economic or personal hardship, people need a hand to get back on their feet. Investing in things like employment insurance and health care pays us back in lower crime rates and healthier citizens.

41. A member of the Conservative Party of Canada would **most likely** agree with which of the given speakers?

  A. Speaker I

  B. Speaker II

  C. Speaker III

  D. Speaker IV

42. Speaker I is **most likely** a member of

  A. the Green party

  B. the Liberal party

  C. the Conservative party

  D. the New Democratic Party

43. Which of the speakers is focusing **primarily** on an area of provincial rights and responsibilities?

  A. Speaker I

  B. Speaker II

  C. Speaker III

  D. Speaker IV

Use the following source to answer the next two questions.

Statement made by a prime minister about Canadian Northern economic development

Obviously, when you excavate the ground here, you create some environmental issues. It must be stated that these issues cannot stop development. If we would not stop development in Toronto, Montreal, or Vancouver, we will not stop development in the North. Our government remains focussed on the economy and job growth. This means expanding new opportunities, and innovators need to be free to develop the North to bring real economic opportunities and long-term local jobs.

Statement made in response to the statement above by an opposition politician

We know that the government emphasizes economic gains over environmental impacts. This statement is surprising and deeply troubling, and our party clearly opposes the government's approach. This policy is short-sighted, and because environmental impacts of mining are so numerous, we can't turn our backs on these concerns and forge ahead without thinking about them. Any development must be done in a sustainable and environmentally responsible way.

44. Where on the political spectrum does the prime minister **most likely** fit?

   A. In the centre

   B. Left of centre

   C. Right of centre

   D. Extreme left of centre

45. The **main** issue represented in this source is

   A. economic sustainability versus the environment

   B. economic development versus the environment

   C. northern jobs versus jobs in southern Canada

   D. government plans versus opposition reaction

Questions 46 to 60 do not require the use of any sources.

46. Which of the following characteristics is **not** present in a liberal democracy?

   A. Periodic free elections

   B. Citizens subject to the rule of law

   C. Government control over the economy

   D. Constitutionally guaranteed rights and freedoms

47. Adam Smith's economic theories were a direct challenge to the practices of
    A. feudalism
    B. communism
    C. mercantilism
    D. industrialism

48. The Cuban Missile Crisis occurred when
    A. the Americans threatened to launch missiles at Cuba
    B. spy planes captured images of missile bases in Cuba
    C. a CIA-backed invasion discovered missile bases in Cuba
    D. the Soviets demanded the removal of American missile bases from Cuba

49. The lessening of hostilities between the superpowers after the Cuban Missile crisis was known as
    A. detente
    B. glasnost
    C. deterrence
    D. containment

50. A command economy is one in which the government
    A. controls key industries and utilities
    B. has complete control over the economy
    C. lets collectives determine the course of the economy
    D. lets market forces determine the course of the economy

51. What was the **main** purpose of the War Measures Act?
    A. It allowed the government to conscript citizens.
    B. It allowed the government to suspend civil liberties.
    C. It allowed the government to declare war on Germany.
    D. It allowed the government to institute wartime rationing.

52. A referendum is an example of
    A. direct democracy
    B. liberal democracy
    C. deliberative democracy
    D. representative democracy

53. Which of the following statements is the reason was the Canadian government was able to intern citizens during the First and Second World Wars?

    A. The government invoked the War Measures Act

    B. The provinces invoked the notwithstanding clause

    C. The government declared them to be enemy aliens

    D. The Charter of Rights and Freedoms had not yet been created

54. For which of the following bills could the notwithstanding clause be used?

    A. A bill making it illegal to picket government buildings in Ontario

    B. A bill exempting all citizens of British Columbia from paying the GST

    C. A bill denying prisoners the right to vote in provincial elections in Alberta

    D. A bill forbidding citizens from Manitoba from immigrating to Saskatchewan

55. To prevent a pandemic, the Canadian government could take all of the following actions **except**

    A. vaccinating citizens against infection

    B. placing infected persons in quarantine

    C. expelling infected persons from the country

    D. discouraging travel to and from high-risk nations

56. In which Warsaw Pact nation did the Solidarity movement topple the Communist regime?

    A. Poland

    B. Romania

    C. East Germany

    D. Czechoslovakia

57. Which of the following individuals is **most closely** associated with *supply side* economies?

    A. Karl Marx

    B. Adam Smith

    C. John Stuart Mill

    D. John Maynard Keynes

58. When wealth is redistributed in a society via universal social programs it represents values linked to

    A. capitalism

    B. egalitarianism

    C. neoconservatism

    D. classical liberalism

59. Laissez-faire capitalism is **most** similar to

    A. Social Darwinism

    B. Utopian socialism

    C. Modern liberalism

    D. Marxist communism

60. The Warsaw Pact was created in response to the

    A. building of the Berlin Wall

    B. dictates of the Truman Doctrine

    C. monetary conditions imposed by the Marshall Plan

    D. existence of the North Atlantic Treaty Organization

ANSWERS AND SOLUTIONS—PRACTICE TEST 1

1.	B	13.	D	25.	A	37.	C	49.	A
2.	D	14.	D	26.	B	38.	B	50.	B
3.	D	15.	B	27.	B	39.	A	51.	B
4.	A	16.	A	28.	C	40.	B	52.	A
5.	D	17.	C	29.	B	41.	B	53.	A
6.	A	18.	D	30.	A	42.	A	54.	A
7.	C	19.	A	31.	C	43.	C	55.	C
8.	B	20.	D	32.	A	44.	C	56.	A
9.	B	21.	D	33.	D	45.	B	57.	B
10.	B	22.	D	34.	B	46.	C	58.	B
11.	B	23.	C	35.	D	47.	C	59.	A
12.	C̶ B	24.	B	36.	A	48.	B	60.	D

1. B

The rule of law means that no person, up to and including heads of state, is above the nation's laws. In a nation without the rule of law, a government official might escape punishment for a crime.

2. D

Freedom of assembly is one of the cornerstones of a free and democratic society. The headline helps illustrate this. The numbers mean that they must be able to do so freely; illegal protests of that size occur only rarely and are generally directed against the government itself.

3. D

Communist, totalitarian, and monarchic states might permit the situation described in *The Daily*. However, controversy and protest are not welcome in such states, and the rule of law is, at best, imperfectly applied. Therefore, only in a liberal democracy would all of the headlines appear.

4. A

Position I outlines many of the ideas that were outlined by Marx. He advocated centralization of the economy by the government so that all citizens would share in economic prosperity of a country. Since Marx believed that economics was the foundation of society this quote mirrors Marxist beliefs.

5. D

Position II argues that there should be as little government intervention in the economy as possible. It states that competition is more efficient and produces lower costs to society. This is the description of a classical liberal ideology and therefore the only correct response.

6. A

Speaker I automatically assumes that the mainstream viewpoint is the best and that Aboriginal Peoples will fail at self-government.

7. **C**

Referendums refer decisions to the people. This is what Speaker II is referring to; the citizens deciding the outcome of an issue. The speaker suggests that no matter the vote it will be respected and this is a hallmark of referendums.

8. **B**

Speaker III is expressing frustration at the lack of understanding of the First Nations (aboriginal) situation. The Red Paper, written in 1970, was a response by First Nations peoples to plans by the Canadian Government at the time to change their situation. In the paper First Nations Peoples argued that they should be allowed to determine their own priorities and their own future.

9. **B**

This political cartoon illustrates the fact that First Nations issues are very complicated and are not easily and readily dealt with. This is shown through the notion of a unified First Nations society being of the same house but split into various parts. To complicate the situation the various levels of government are also being shown as a split group and not a unified group.

10. **B**

Through the representation of the split house in the cartoon and the various points of view presented by the speakers it can easily be seen that Aboriginal Peoples are incorrectly presumed to be a unified group.

11. **B**

All the speakers are concerned with the interaction between government and citizens in society: namely, what governments provide citizens in exchange for their allegiance. This falls under the category of social contract theory.

12. **¢ B**

Both Speakers II and III are arguing that society needs government to provide stability and safety for its citizens. They are both saying that there is an essential for government in the lives of everyday citizens.

13. **D**

Rousseau believed that citizens should make the laws directly. This represented his view that the general will of the people was the absolute authority. As such, this is what Speaker IV is talking about.

14. **D**

Poor working conditions, filthy urban living conditions, and new technology are all part of the Industrial Revolution, which first arose in England.

Industrialism came after mercantilism was more or less finished, and was spurred by the capitalist economic philosophy that replaced mercantilism. Communism (and socialism in general) was a response to the changes wrought by industrialization.

15. **B**

Given the poor working conditions of the time and the concentration of people in the cities, labourers began to organize into unions.

Most workers could not afford passage to America, and there were few jobs to be had in rural areas. They were not able to gain political power until they had formed unions, which gave them more clout in labour and political disputes.

16. **A**

Both the Nazis and the Communist replaced unpopular regimes in their time. The Nazis eventually replaced the Weimer Government and the Communists replaced the Czarist regime which was equally unpopular with the citizens of Russia.

17. C

The Communists in Russia eventually seized power through a popular revolution that was supported by many Russians.

The Nazis achieved power through a combination election victory and manipulation of their system of government.

18. D

Despite what they may have proclaimed neither the Nazis nor the Communists provided for the welfare of all of their citizens. The Communists, especially under Stalin, oppressed various groups including the Kulaks and the Nazis oppressed the Jews in particular and some other groups as well.

19. A

One of the cornerstones of any totalitarian regime that wants to maintain power is the use of a secret police force. The secret police, through the brutal actions, help maintain dictators in power. Both Hitler and Stalin used the secret police extensively to maintain power through brutal repression of its citizens.

20. D

A representative democracy is one in which the citizens elect people to represent their interests in government, which is what Alejandra is participating in.

In a direct democracy, citizens vote directly on issues. In a deliberative democracy, representatives make decisions after carefully considering input from citizens. A liberal democracy can include any of these decision-making methods.

21. D

In 1946, soon after the end of the Second World War, the Soviets had a large military presence in Eastern Europe. This enabled them to establish Communist regimes in nations such as Poland, Czechoslovakia, Hungary, and Romania. The new Soviet-controlled buffer zone between democratic Western Europe and the Soviet Union is Churchill's "iron curtain."

The Warsaw Pact was not signed until 1955; construction on the Berlin Wall began in 1961.

22. D

Former general secretary Brezhnev is saying that Communist nations should do whatever they can to prevent other Communist nations from adopting liberalization or capitalism, even if it means violating their sovereignty. He made this statement following the Soviet Union's use of military force to prevent liberal reforms in Czechoslovakia.

23. C

The Berlin Wall was a symbol of the restriction on free movement to and from Warsaw Pact nations. By asking former general secretary of the Soviet Union Gorbachev to "tear down this wall," former president Reagan is asking for the elimination of these restrictions.

24. B

The given sources refer to the establishment, maintenance, and eventual collapse of the Soviet Union's sphere of influence.

25. A

All three speakers were speaking during and about the time known as the Cold War. Winston Churchill was speaking at the start of this time period and Ronald Reagan was speaking near the end of the Cold War.

26. B

Speaker I emphasizes efficiency and quick action over free debate and the will of the people; thus, Speaker I likely supports a totalitarian government.

27. B

Both Communist and democratic governments try to ensure the greatest good for the greatest number, but they differ in how they go about doing so. Communist governments enforce economic equality among citizens, while democratic governments provide their citizens with guaranteed rights and freedoms.

28. C

Speaker III wants minimum government interference. Higher taxes, nationalization of industry, and new tariffs are all examples of government interference.

29. B

Adam Smith, along with many classical liberals, would support the first response on the chart because this is an area that they believed government should be involved in. Smith would argue that one of the only roles a government should have is to provide protection in a society. This is a generality and there will always be specifics that might preclude this as being true.

The other three people listed in the question were not really concerned with specific government action and dealt more with the overarching ideas of citizens and government.

30. A

The correct response is the only one that directly relates to how people and their governments could relate and interact.

The three other answers either deal with only part of the population being interviewed or deal with how citizens can be involved with government and not how government can meet the needs of the people.

31. C

The primary purpose of the residential school system was to eliminate Aboriginal cultures by educating Aboriginal children in European culture, religion, history and so forth.

32. A

Despite the best efforts of the residential school system, Aboriginal groups have managed to preserve their culture and traditions, and are working hard to pass them on to younger generations. In his 2008 address, Prime Minister Harper specifically apologizes for the individual trauma, damages to families, and damage to Aboriginal communities caused by the residential school system.

33. D

On September 22, 1988, Prime Minister Brian Mulroney issued a formal apology to Japanese Canadians who were interned during World War II as enemy aliens. This apology was similar to the apology over Residential Schools.

The other three choices have not yet happened at the present.

34. B

The image in the cartoon shows that the First Nations Peoples are still affected by the Residential School situation. This is shown through the First Nations person having a ball and chain around his ankle and the words "Residential Schools" on the ball. As well, while the prime minister is looking content and his speech indicates that the situation is behind them the First Nations person has a sad and resigned look on him.

35. D

The words as spoken by the prime minister show that he believes that everything has been looked after with regards to the Residential School situation. The indications are that what the prime minister has carried out is sufficient to bring about a resolution to the situation. The truth is that it is far from that as reflected in the First Nations person in the cartoon.

36. A

One of the fundamental rights of Canadian citizens is freedom of thought. Canadians cannot be punished for what they think or believe (expressing or acting on those beliefs and thoughts may be a different story, though).

A Supreme Court judge would know better than to propose fining people for their beliefs.

37. C

In 1989, the Quebec government used the notwithstanding clause to pass such a law; that law has since been amended to comply with the Charter of Rights and Freedoms.

Language rights are part of the Canadian Constitution. Although Quebec does have its own charter, Canada's charter takes precedence.

38. B

Under the Emergencies Act the can step in and deal with a public welfare emergency that deals with diseases in humans, animals or plants. As such, the Express headline is perfectly possible in Canada.

39. A

The overall tone and direction of this article is one that argues that the Canadian government went too far in dealing with the issue of terrorism after 9-11. The article states that the legislation is too broad and the powers that the government has are too far reaching. Essentially it is arguing that people's rights are being trampled in the name of dealing with terrorism.

40. B

The viewpoint of this article excerpt is that of a socialist viewpoint. It is this because it is reacting to a conservative implementation of a curbing of rights in order to combat terrorism. It mentions the fact that trade unionists could even be seen as terrorists in certain conditions.

41. B

The Conservative Party of Canada strongly supports increased military spending.

42. A

The Green Party of Canada strongly supports environmental protection and believes that it can be done without seriously burdening the economy.

43. C

Speaker II is focusing mainly on education which is a provincial matter in Canada. While everything this speaker is saying may be true, the ideas are all dealing with an issue that only the individual provinces can deal with.

44. C

Because the prime minister that is speaking is focusing on development and economic expansion in various areas in Canada, specifically the North, he represents a right of centre view. This is because people with this view focus first on the jobs and development and then on the environment. He represents the traditional classical liberal view.

45. B

The statements by both speakers represent a view of jobs versus the environment. The prime minister advocates that jobs should come first before a major focus on the environment and the second speaker is suggesting that this is not the proper tact to take and that it is the environment that should take precedence over industrial expansion.

46. C

Liberal democracies normally employ mixed economies-free market capitalism with limited government interference. Government control over the economy is a collectivist characteristic; it would most likely be found in a socialist or Communist nation, not in a liberal democracy.

47. C

Most European nations in Smith's day were mercantilist, and it is mercantilist practices that Smith overturns in *The Wealth of Nations*.

48. B

On October 14, 1962, American spy planes took pictures of missile bases being built in Cuba. Cuba was (and is) a Communist nation, and its close proximity to the United States meant that it could easily hit American cities with ordinary or nuclear missiles.

49. A

Detente is a French word meaning "relaxation or easing."

Glasnost was former general secretary of the Soviet Union Gorbachev's policy of political openness. Deterrence, in the given context, means to prevent attack by being strong enough to seriously hurt or destroy any attacking force. Containment was the American policy of preventing the spread of communism beyond the established Soviet sphere of influence.

50. B

As the name suggests, the conduct of the economy is done at the command of the government. This means that the government has complete control over the production and distribution of goods.

Command economies are the opposite of free market economies, in which the government lets market forces determine the course of the economy.

51. B

The War Measures Act allowed the government to suspend civil liberties during times of conflict, such as war or rebellion.

52. A

A referendum is when a government asks citizens to vote directly on a piece of legislation, such as a constitutional amendment. It is an example of direct democracy.

53. A

The War Measures Act allowed the government to suspend civil liberties. This gave them the power to intern citizens whose ancestors came from enemy nations.

The notwithstanding clause did not exist yet and would not apply here in any case. It is true that the Charter of Rights and Freedoms did not exist yet, but citizens still had fundamental liberal-democratic rights.

54. A

Although such a bill would be terribly unpopular, the Ontario government could, in theory, use the notwithstanding clause to interfere with people's freedom of assembly.

The GST (Goods and Services Tax) is a federal tax, so the British Columbia government could not pass laws about it. The right to vote is a democratic right and cannot be circumvented with the notwithstanding clause, Canadian citizens may choose to live in any province or territory; the notwithstanding clause cannot be used to infringe on mobility rights.

55. C

Expelling infected persons would be irresponsible at best, and, in the case of citizens, a major violation of constitutional rights. Whether or not the infected person was a citizen, the government would ensure that the individual received treatment and would not spread the disease.

56. A

The Solidarity group, under the leadership of Lech Walesa, pressured the Communist government into allowing partially free elections, in which it won an overwhelming victory.

57. B

The underlying aspect of supply side economics is reduced government involvement in the economy and a lowering of taxes. This is also known as trickle-down economics. Since Adam Smith was a supporter of little government involvement in the economy he would be a great supporter of this economic concept.

58. B

Since egalitarianism means that all people should be treated as equals and allowed equal, civil, social, political, and economic rights under the law it supports the concepts of universal social programs.

59. A

The idea between laissez-faire capitalism is that free markets with little government involvement will prevail. The assumption is that the most economically fit companies will survive in an economy based on open competition. This is very similar to Darwin's thoughts in his survival of the fittest theory but applied in an economic situation.

60. D

The North Atlantic Treaty Organization (NATO) was formed as an organization to protect the nations of Western Europe from the threat of a possible attack by the Soviet Union. In response to this perceived threat the Soviet Union created a like organization that consisted of the Soviet East Bloc and the Soviet Union. This was meant to be a deterrent to the threat from the West.

PRACTICE TEST 2

Use the following sources to answer the next three questions.

Source I—Speaker

My parents immigrated to Canada when I was very young. They've always taught me to be proud of who I am and my family's history but lately, we've been arguing a lot about which traditions I have to maintain. I'm almost finished high school and I want to wear fashionable clothes, go to University and date. I'm not interested in marrying some guy my parents choose and having kids right away. In our former country, women have to cover themselves and have considerably fewer freedoms than Canadian women. I love my parents but they don't understand that in Canada being a woman means having choices, a voice and being an equal, contributing part of society.

Source II—Factors Influencing Individual Beliefs and Values

I. Gender

II. Culture

III. Religion

IV. Language

V. Environment

VI. Relationship to the Land

---

1. The speaker in Source I is in a struggle between tradition and

    A. history

    B. fashion

    C. freedom

    D. marriage

2. Which two factors from Source II are most likely in conflict for the speaker?

    A. I and II

    B. I and IV

    C. III and V

    D. III and VI

3. Which of the factors from Source II is **most likely** the source of the beliefs held by the speaker's parents?

   A. III

   B. IV

   C. V

   D. VI

Use the following source to answer the next two questions.

"Yes, well there are a lot of bleeding hearts around who just don't like to see people with helmets and guns. All I can say is, go on and bleed, but it is more important to keep law and order in the society than to be worried about weak-kneed people...I think the society must take every means at its disposal to defend itself against the emergence of a parallel power which defies the elected power in this country and I think that goes to any distance."

—Pierre Trudeau, October 13th, 1970

4. The position taken by Pierre Trudeau in the quotation is that

   A. it is important for a country to have a strong military which can be used during domestic crises

   B. governments should uphold liberalism and respect the individual rights of citizens even during time of crisis

   C. there should be specific limits on the ability of government to restrict the liberties of its citizens during times of crisis

   D. the practices of governments must sometimes reject liberalism in order for the well being of society as a whole to be maintained during times of crisis

5. Which of the following acts would have allowed Prime Minister Trudeau to act in the manner that he described in the given source?

   A. PATRIOT Act

   B. Emergencies Act

   C. War Measures Act

   D. Anti-Terrorism Act

Speaker I

Economic equality is essential if a country is to maintain order among its citizens. All people have a right to a roof over their head and to know they will not be hungry. It shouldn't matter that this equality is not necessarily achieved through labour equality, the collective goal should be to improve society as a whole and if that means some people may contribute more than others, so be it. Classes among society are simply intolerable.

Speaker II

The notion that equality and universal access to all things deemed "necessary" is a basic right is preposterous. The knowledge that someone who works hard day after day will receive the same benefits as someone who doesn't will promote apathy and provides no incentive for personal responsibility. People should have to work for what they have; it should not be handed to them.

Speaker III

In order for society to function at its utmost potential, people need to follow what society expects of them. Although people may have their own opinions and beliefs about political, social, or economic issues, they should understand that a country needs to have a united front. As a result, it is in a country's best interest for its citizens to keep their personal opinions private and support the party line.

Speaker IV

Expecting someone to stay quiet about their deeply held beliefs on serious issues will only result in inevitable revolution. The ability for a person to express their opinions in a peaceful manner, even if it is different from the ideas of the majority is an essential part of a successful society. Human beings do not like to be suppressed and it's important to guarantee that within reason, they won't be. Overall, society will be better for it.

6. The speaker who is **most supportive** of a country's citizens adhering to collective norms is
   A. Speaker I
   B. Speaker II
   C. Speaker III
   D. Speaker IV

7. The speaker who would **most likely** be critical of government-regulated wages to promote wealth equity is
   A. Speaker I
   B. Speaker II
   C. Speaker III
   D. Speaker IV

8. Which of the speakers would **most likely** agree with the statement "From each according to his ability, to each according to his needs"?

A. Speaker I

B. Speaker II

C. Speaker III

D. Speaker IV

Use the following source to answer the next two questions.

9. Which of the following American presidents would agree with the speaker in the cartoon?

A   Bill Clinton

B.   Jimmy Carter

C.   Ronald Reagan

D.   George W. Bush

10. The economic policy referred to in the cartoon is

A. stagflation

B. monetarism

C. command economics

D. supply-side economics

Use the following source to answer the next three questions.

"It took more than a year of partisan bickering, deal making and amendments, but the U.S. Congress has approved sweeping changes to the way health care is delivered in the United States.

Despite the passage of legislation by both the Senate and the House of Representatives, the United States political establishment remains bitterly divided over the American health-care system. The almost $1-trillion bill that will eventually extend coverage to as many as 32 million previously uninsured Americans passed without a single Republican vote.

It's the first time in U.S. history that such a major piece of legislation has been approved solely on the votes of the governing party.

Opponents of the bill derided it as a march to Canadian-style "socialized medicine," arguing that it gives the government too much say over the way health care is delivered.

"This isn't radical reform," U.S. President Barack Obama said after the legislation was approved on March 21, 2010, "but it is major reform."

While the legislation will soon ensure that more people than ever have access to health insurance, the new rules will mean the U.S. remains the only industrialized nation in the world without universal health-care coverage."

11. The bill described in the article is an example of the expression of

A. collectivism within a collectivist society

B. individualism within a collectivist society

C. collectivism within an individualist society

D. individualism within an individualistic society

12. Which of the following quotations from the source **best** illustrates a conflict between those supportive and those critical of collectivist ideas within American society?

A. "Congress has approved sweeping changes to the way health care is delivered in the United States."

B. "The almost $1-trillion bill that will eventually extend coverage to as many as 32 million previously uninsured Americans passed without a single Republican vote. "

C. "It's the first time in U.S. history that such a major piece of legislation has been approved solely on the votes of the governing party."

D. "the new rules will mean the U.S. remains the only industrialized nation in the world without universal health-care coverage."

13. Those opposing the bill in the source would **most likely** be classified as

    A. collectivists

    B. modern liberals

    C. classical liberals

    D. neoconservatives

Use the following source to answer the next two questions.

Example I

The owner of a major stationary supply chain sets up a food bank style outlet for school supplies in a low income area for the month of September.

Example II

A wealthy business owner buys several investment properties in areas where there is a depressed real estate market.

Example III

A traditional agricultural communal society decides to allow some members to obtain employment outside the community.

Example IV

A right wing government decides to eliminate child care subsidies to middle class families.

---

14. The two examples that show **both** the inclusion of collectivist and individualist ideology within society are

    A. examples I and II

    B. examples I and III

    C. examples II and IV

    D. examples III and IV

15. Which of the examples listed **most likely** describes a person or society that would consider providing for the common good the main priority?

    A. Example I

    B. Example II

    C. Example III

    D. Example IV

Use the following source to answer the next three questions.

Speaker 1

Protecting the environment is important to me. I'm glad our government has been working with other governments to find solutions to some of the biggest problems our planet faces. I have faith that our leaders will be able to put together plans that will maintain our standards of living while improving our relationship with the Earth.

Speaker II

I understand that the environment is important but so is my ability to put food on my table and buy clothes for my kids. I don't think the government should be able to restrict a flourishing industry to save a few trees. People will make the right decisions without someone telling them how to do it.

Speaker III

Each summit, each accord, each claim made by governments over the past decade have meant nothing. It's time for governments to exert real change in their societies. Obviously, the only way people are going to change is if they are forced to and unfortunately we've come to the breaking point – the environment will soon be damaged beyond repair without major change.

Speaker IV

I think I do pretty well by the environment. I recycle; I've tried to consume less and developed new habits like using a reusable bottle instead of buying bottled water. However, I value the fact that I've made these decisions myself. Although I think the government needs to make rules for major polluters in industry, I think I would resent it if the government started telling me what to do and how to live.

16. Which of the following speakers presents an opinion that poses the **greatest** challenge to modern liberalism?

   A. Speaker I

   B. Speaker II

   C. Speaker III

   D. Speaker IV

17. Which of the following two speakers present the **most varied** opinions about the need for government intervention in order to protect the environment?

   A. Speakers I and II

   B. Speakers I and IV

   C. Speakers II and III

   D. Speakers III and IV

18.　Which of the following speakers would **most likely** be classified as classical liberals?

   A. Speakers I and II

   B. Speakers I and III

   C. Speakers II and IV

   D. Speakers III and IV

Use the following source to answer the next two questions.

Source I

Syncrude, a large oilsands company, is facing charges because more than 1 000 birds died after landing in the company's Aurora tailings pond. A tailings pond is where discarded waste from oilsands activity is mixed with water and companies are required to have noise making deterrents to prevent birds and animals from mistaking the area for a safe source of water. The deterrent equipment at the Aurora pond was not in working order when the large group of birds landed there in April 2008.

Source II

19. Taken together Source I and Source II are both referring to which of the following ideological themes?

   A. Religious beliefs

   B. Class differences

   C. Economic freedom

   D. Relationship to the land

20. The message in Source II, the cartoon, is that

   A. corporate profit is less important than the environment

   B. corporate profit is more important than the environment

   C. corporations balance profit with treatment of the environment

   D. corporations are good civic citizens with regards to the environment

Use the following source to answer the next three questions.

"More trucks kept coming, one after another, unloading American soldiers and military police with rifles who began canvassing the neighborhood, nailing small posters to doors, storefronts, and telephone poles. Merchants and customers alike poured out to see the commotion. Henry and the Okabes stepped onto the sidewalk as soldiers walked past, handing out copies of the flyer –"Public Proclamation I," which was written in English and Japanese.

Henry looked at the paper in Keiko's hand. The bold type screamed; INSTRUCTIONS TO ALL PERSONS OF JAPANESE ANCESTRY. It was all about Japanese families being forced to evacuate, for their own safety. They had only a few days and could bring next to nothing – only what they could carry. At the bottom, it was signed by the president of the United States and the secretary of war."

—from Hotel on the Corner of Bitter and Sweet by Jamie Ford

21. The situation described in the excerpt took place during which of the following events?

A. Korean War

B. First World War

C. Afghanistan War

D. Second World War

22. The events described in the excerpt are an example of

A. a liberal government upholding its principles

B. a non-liberal government upholding its policies

C. a liberal government contradicting its principles

D. a non-liberal government contradicting its policies

23. Which Canadian government action was similar to the one described in the source?

A. The operation of Residential Schools

B. The arrest and detention of terror suspects after 9/11

C. The interment of Ukrainian Canadians during the First World War

D. The expulsion from Canada of FLQ members during the October Crisis

Use the following source to answer the next two questions.

The Daily

Charter Trumps Education Act Over Prayers

TORONTO—The rights of Muslim students to have midday Islamic prayer sessions in their public schools tumps Ontario's rules around education, according to a statement from the Toronto District School Board.

Weekly Weather
M T W T F S S

24. Which Canadian piece of legislation is referred to in the headline used in the source?

   A. Bill of Rights

   B. Emergencies Act

   C. Constitutional Act

   D. Charter of Rights and Freedoms

25. Which of the following countries would **most likely** prevent the action in the article from taking place?

   A. Italy, because only one religion is allowed

   B. Great Britain, because public prayer is not allowed

   C. Germany, because it does not recognize immigrant's rights

   D. France, because it preserves the secular character of public institutions

Speaker I I believe that every individual is free to do as he or she chooses, so long as the individual's actions do not harm others.
Speaker II I believe that people should work for themselves in a free market system.
Speaker III I believe that all economic endeavours should be made to benefit the state.
Speaker IV I believe that all people must be ruled and governed by an absolute monarch.

26. Which of the given speakers would **most likely** oppose mercantilism?

    A. Speaker I

    B. Speaker II

    C. Speaker III

    D. Speaker IV

27. Which of the following individuals would **most likely** have agreed with the statement made by Speaker II?

    A. John Locke

    B. Adam Smith

    C. Thomas Hobbes

    D. Baron de Montesquieu

28. John Steward Mill would **most likely** have agreed with the statement made by

    A. Speaker I

    B. Speaker II

    C. Speaker III

    D. Speaker IV

Use the following source to answer the next two questions.

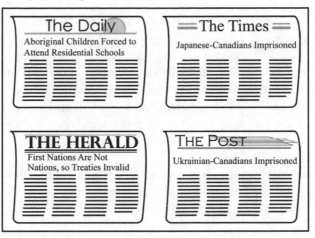

29. Which of the following issues **most directly** relates to the headlines of all four newspapers?

   A. To what extent should governments reflect the will of the people?

   B. To what extent should governments impose the principles of liberalism?

   C. To what extent do liberal democracies reflect illiberal thought and practices?

   D. To what extent should government balance the needs of society with the rights of the individual?

30. The headline from which newspaper describes an event that Prime Minister Stephen Harper formally apologized for in 2008?

   A. *The Post*

   B. *The Daily*

   C. *The Times*

   D. *The Herald*

Use the following source to answer the next three questions.

Views on Changes to the Wheat Board

Canadian Government Politician

It is time to stop the monopoly of the Canadian Wheat Board in Western Canada. The removal of the monopoly will allow western farmers to sell directly to the grain handlers instead of marketing those crops only through the Board. We will still support the Board for the next five years and then they will have to compete with other companies.

Canadian Farmer I

I'm going to see more companies want to buy my grain. The more competition the better. Things will be better for farmers under open competition.

Canadian Farmer II

This move is anti-democratic becausee the government wants to remove farmer-elected directors from the Board and replace them with government appointees. We farmers have elected them and the government is going to remove them. What they are doing is illegal.

31. The Canadian government politician would **most likely** be a supporter of

   A. neoconservatism

   B. utopian socialism

   C. modern liberalism

   D. classical liberalism

32.   Farmer I supports the government's action because it will give him

   A. more choice

   B. less competition

   C. guaranteed prices

   D. increased markets

33. Farmer II has objections that are based on his belief that the government is being

   A. liberal

   B. illiberal

   C. democratic

   D. authoritarian

Use the following source to answer the next two questions.

34. The cartoon represents the government action of dismantling the Canadian Wheat Board as an action that is

   A. uncaring

   B. calculated

   C. consultative

   D. well-planned

35. The action of the railcar in the cartoon shows that the Canadian Wheat Board is

   A. plunging into the unknown

   B. headed in a positive direction

   C. unlikely to survive in the future

   D. going to be around for a long time

Use the following source to answer the next three questions.

Speaker I

I believe in violent revolution to overthrow the government to stop the growth of liberalism. I believe the government should be organized using collective units that work toward a command economy. I instituted the New Economic Policy.

Speaker II

I ended the New Economic Policy and implemented strict collectivization using five-year plans. The entire political system was in my hands and that of my Communist bureaucracy. Goods were distributed according to the needs of the state and the five-year plans. I also purged any opposition to my leadership.

Speaker III

I created the National Socialist German Workers' Party, which exploited the people's frustration with the Treaty of Versailles at the end of the First World War. I believed my fellow countrymen were naturally superior to all other peoples. I used violence and intimidation to control and to rid my country of the "sub-humans."

Speaker IV

I lived through the horrors of forced collectivization, famine, and millions of unnecessary deaths. The lives of my fellow people were of less importance than the government and the wealth of the state.

36. Which speaker was **most likely** responsible for the deaths of six million Ukrainians?

    A. Speaker I

    B. Speaker II

    C. Speaker III

    D. Speaker IV

37. Vladimir Lenin and Adolf Hitler are **best** represented by which of the following speakers?

    A. Speakers I and II

    B. Speakers III and IV

    C. Speakers I and III

    D. Speakers II and IV

38. Speaker IV is referring to which event?

    A. The Holocaust

    B. The Holodomor

    C. The First World War

    D. The Second World War

Use the following source to answer the next two questions.

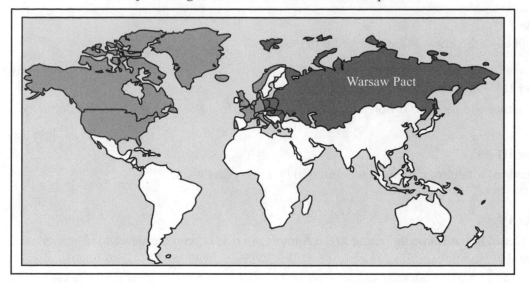

39. The shaded unnamed countries on the world map are known collectively as

   A. NATO

   B. NORAD

   C. the WTO

   D. the WHO

40. Many of the countries that are **not** shaded on the map joined to form the

   A. Non-Aligned Movement

   B. Project for the New American Century

   C. Organisation international de la Francophonie

   D. Organization of the Petroleum Exporting Countries

Use the following source to answer the next three questions.

Speaker I

"We walked to the brink and we looked it in the face."

—John Foster Dulles

Speaker II

"If we cannot end now our differences, at least we can help make the world safe for diversity."

—John F. Kennedy

Speaker III

"The seeds of totalitarian regimes are nurtured by misery and want."

—Harry S. Truman

Speaker IV

"From Stettin in the Baltic to Trieste in the Adriatic, an iron curtain has descended across the continent."

—Winston Churchill

41. Speaker I is most likely referring to

   A. dissuasion

   B. proliferation

   C. containment

   D. brinkmanship

42. Speaker II is **most likely** referring to

   A. detente

   B. deterrence

   C. expansionism

   A. nonalignment

43. What are all three speakers **most likely** talking about?

   A. Fascist Italy

   B. Nazi Germany

   C. Communist Russia

   D. Democratic America

Use the following additional source to answer the next two questions.

44. The figure speaking in the cartoon is **most likely** referring to

    A. deterrence

    B. containment

    C. proliferation

    D. brinkmanship

45. Taken together, both the quotes and the cartoon are dealing with the

    A. Cold War

    B. Korean War

    C. Vietnam War

    D. Second World War

Questions 46 to 60 do not require any sources.

46. The attempt to find more efficient methods of production during the Industrial Revolution was rooted in

    A. the growing focus on creating high quality versus high quantity goods

    B. the inherent value in commodities and the labour needed to produce them

    C. the shifting beliefs about the importance of providing a safe working environment for labourers

    D. the belief that people would work harder if they believed they were contributing to something worthwhile

47. Which of the following ideas would **best** correspond with the beliefs of Edmond Burke?

A. Preventing new ideas and no change

B. Maintaining the status quo or slow change

C. Returning to old traditions and societal norms

D. Supporting radical change politically and economically

48. Which of the following statements would **least likely** be supported by John Stuart Mill?

A. Free speech is a necessary part of a liberal, democratic society.

B. People should be free to act as they please as long as their actions are not detrimental to others.

C. Government must provide protection for those who are in the minority of thought, race or other provision.

D. Due to their inherent differences, men and women cannot play an equal role in society and the political decision-making process.

49. Limited government involvement, few or no social programs and an expectation of self sufficiency are all characteristics of

A. mixed economies

B. command economies

C. traditional economies

D. free market economies

50. Which of the following groups exhibited unity among nations, equal participation of all people and division of power between different levels of government?

A. The Canadian Confederacy

B. The American rebolutionaries

C. The Haudenosaunee Confedarcy

D. The French monarchy of the 18th century

51. Which of the following individuals believed that if change had to come about it had to honour the citizens of the past and the future?

A. Karl Marx

B. Adam Smith

C. Robert Owen

D. Edmund Burke

52. In Canada, which of the following laws or rights overrides all others?

   A. A City of Edmonton bylaw

   B. A Government of Alberta piece of legislation

   C. The Canadian Charter of Rights and Freedoms

   D. The Québec Charter of Human Rights and Freedoms

53. John Stuart Mill would be **most** associated with which of the following statements?

   A. Individuals should be free to act as they wish so long as those actions are not detrimental to others

   B. Government should contain a separation of powers to prevent any one part of government from abusing its powers

   C. The economy will work to its full potential when people are given the freedom to pursue their own self interest with very few government restraints

   D. In exchange for social order and individual freedoms, citizens should be prepared to surrender some of their decision making to a government which is accountable

54. Jean-Jacques Rousseau would be **most** associated with which of the following statements?

   A. People are rational, reasonable, and intelligent and government exists solely to protect life, liberty, and property

   B. People are inherently good and free and every citizen should have a voice in the government and in the creation of laws

   C. An absolute monarchy is wrong and all people should be equal, represented by an accountable, democratic government

   D. While people are not evil, they are selfish, and need to voluntarily surrender their individual freedoms to the state to ensure the security of all citizens

55. Which of the following statements would a critic of the Canadian parliamentary system **most likely** agree with?

   A. Canada's voters must be 18 years of age to vote.

   B. Canadian senators are appointed and not elected.

   C. Canadian provinces cannot pass laws about education.

   D. Canada's prime minister can hold office for an unlimited number of terms.

56. The period of reduced tensions, from the mid-1960's to 1979, was called

   A. detente

   B. alignment

   C. deterrence

   D. brinkmanship

57. The goal of the Truman Doctrine was the
    A. dissuasion of Soviet nuclear attacks
    B. non-alignment of Soviet satellite states
    C. expansion of the Soviet sphere of influence
    D. containment of Soviet communist influence

58. In 1949, NATO was created by the West as
    A. an organization to help the Soviet Union after the Second World War
    B. a military alliance designed to defend against attach from the Soviet Union
    C. a group of nations to work with the Soviet Union in nuclear disarmament talks
    D. an early warning system by the United States to monitor incoming missiles from the Soviet Union

59. Whose economic theories brought about the economic thinking that is referred to as Reaganomics?
    A. Karl Marx
    B. Adam Smith
    C. Milton Friedman
    D. John Maynard Keynes

60. Which of the following Soviet actions or events is **not** associated with Joseph Stalin?
    A. Five Year Plans
    D. The Holodomor
    C. Collectivization
    D. The New Economic Policy

ANSWERS AND SOLUTIONS—PRACTICE TEST 2

1.	C	13.	C	25.	D	37.	B̸ C	49.	D
2.	A	14.	B	26.	B	38.	B	50.	C
3.	A	15.	C	27.	B	39.	A	51.	D
4.	D	16.	C	28.	A	40.	A	52.	C
5.	C	17.	C	29.	C	41.	D	53.	A
6.	C	18.	C	30.	B	42.	A	54.	B
7.	B	19.	D	31.	D	43.	C	55.	B
8.	A	20.	B	32.	A	44.	A	56.	A
9.	C	21.	D	33.	B	45.	A	57.	D
10.	D	22.	C	34.	A	46.	B	58.	B
11.	C	23.	C	35.	C	47.	B	59.	C
12.	B	24.	D	36.	B	48.	D	60.	D

1. C

The speaker is in a struggle between tradition and freedom.

The speaker wants to enjoy the freedoms of her new homeland and not be saddled with the traditions of the family culture. In other words the speaker wants to be a free citizen in Canada and not be restricted by the expectations of parents and tradition.

2. A

The speaker is conflicted between the gender differences that exist between Canadian culture and her family's cultural expectations.

The speaker is not addressing issues to do with the environment, language or relationship to the land. Although religion may be a factor in the speaker's parent's culture, it is not addressed specifically by the speaker.

3. A

The way the speaker depicts the role of women in her parents' home country is likely influenced by religion.

In some countries and cultures gender equality is viewed differently and these differences are sometimes justified through claims of religious mandate from religious texts. Men and women around the world who share the same religion interpret the writings of these books differently and may hold differing views on issues such as the rights of women.

4. D

In this famous quotation, Pierre Trudeau states his position : the government needs to take all necessary means to protect the well-being of society when there is a threat or crisis.

He does not discuss the need for a strong military. His position suggests he would be supportive of limiting individual rights and giving government considerable power to restrict civil liberties during times of crisis in order to protect the collective.

5. **C**

   During the October Crisis in the early 1970's, the only legislation Prime Minister Trudeau had to use was the War Measures Act. It allowed him to deal with the perceived threat that faced Canada at the time.

   None of the other pieces of legislation listed were in effect during the 1970s and the PATRIOT Act is an American piece of legislation.

6. **C**

   Speaker III states that even if someone disagrees with a decision being made in a country, that person should adhere to collective norms and not express his/her disagreement.

   Speakers I and II do not discuss adherence to collective norms and Speaker IV suggests that the expectation of adherence to collective norms is detrimental to society as a whole.

7. **B**

   Speaker II suggests that the government should not be responsible for wealth equity and people should be paid according to their work. As a result, government regulated wages would likely be something about which the speaker would be critical.

   Speaker I would likely support regulated wages because it would help reduce wealthy inequity. Speakers III and IV do not discuss issues related to wealth equity.

8. **A**

   Speaker I suggests that economic equality should exist in society and that in order to achieve this equality, people must accept that work will not be equal and people will contribute what they can. This is also the basis of Karl Marx's quote which means that if everyone contributes according to their abilities, everyone will have access to what they need.

Speaker II would likely disagree with the quote. Speakers III and IV do not discuss issues surrounding economic equality.

9. **C**

   President Ronald Reagan is most associated with trickle - down economics. This economic theory holds that by lowering tax rates, especially for those who are likely to invest capital that economic growth will be encouraged and jobs will be created.

10. **D**

    The trickle down economics referred to in the cartoon is also known as supply side economics. The terms are interchangeable because they both hold that jobs will be created if investors are taxed less so they can invest in the economy and allow for employment.

    The other choices are not related to the cartoon at all. While monetarism comes from the same time it focuses on the control of the money supply through interest rates not through lowering tax rates.

11. **C**

    The United States is an individualist society but the health care reform bill described in the source will provide health care coverage to Americans who previously did not have access to it. This type of government involvement is based in collectivist ideology.

    The other options are incorrect because the United States is not a collectivist society and government involvement is not based in individualist ideology.

12. **B**

    The Republican party of the United States is characterized by holding individualist ideals and is not supportive of the Democratic government actions rooted in collectivist ideals such as increased government control over health care.

The other quotes provide information about the bill but do not suggest a conflict between different groups in the United States.

13. **C**

   Classical liberals would oppose this bill because they believe that choice is being taken away from people.

   They might also oppose this bill because of the government involvement in this process. Classical liberals believe there should be limited government involvement in people's lives and they would view this as an intrusion into people's lives.

14. **B**

   Example I describes how someone who likely holds an individualist ideology is using personal success to provide for the common good. Example III describes a collectivist society that acknowledges some advantage to the individualist perspective.

   Examples II and IV describe people and a society for whom the common good does not appear to be a priority.

15. **C**

   Example III describes a communal community. Such communities generally support the ideals of collectivism through traditions and methods which ensures that all members of the society are provided what they need.

   Examples I, II and IV each describe a person or society that would consider self advancement or the expectation of self-reliance, the primary goal.

16. **C**

   Speaker III suggests that the government must take action to force change in its citizens in order to protect the environment. Modern liberalism does not support such intense government involvement in the lives of its citizens.

   Although the other speakers present varying opinions, none of them present ideas that are in great conflict with the ideas of modern liberalism.

17. **C**

   Speaker II does not support any government regulation in regards to environmental protection while Speaker III feels that the only way to protect the environment is to for the government to introduce regulations.

   Speaker I feels the government will be able to find a balance between regulation and individual freedoms and Speaker IV feels regulation in industry is important but not on individual citizens.

18. **C**

   Speakers II and IV would both be classified as classical liberals but for different reasons. Speaker II is a classical liberal because the speaker believes that there should be limited government involvement in personal life and jobs should be a priority over the environment. On the other hand , Speaker IV is also a classical liberal because the speaker believes it should be the individual , not the government, who determines what their role in the environment. This speaker does advocate some government involvement in the environment but only minimally.

19. **D**

   Both sources are suggesting that the company Syncrude is more concerned with its potential profits from oil sands activity than the environment.

The cartoon does not include the themes of economic freedom, class or religion.

20. B

The person in the cartoon represents the focus of companies on profit rather than the environment. The oil covered duck being held by the duck represents this idea.

21. D

The excerpt is describing the internment of Japanese Americans and also Japanese Canadians which took place during the Second World War.

This internment did not take place during World War I, the Korean War or the Afghanistan War.

22. C

The United States and also Canada are liberalist countries that believe in upholding individual rights. However, the actions taken by these governments to intern citizens of Japanese descent during the Second World War were contradictory to such beliefs.

23. C

During the First World War Canadians who were of German or Ukrainian descent were also interned in camps because of the fear that they might support the enemy and commit acts detrimental to the country.

There were a number of these individuals who did not gain their freedom until as late as 1920. When the same situation faced Japanese-Canadians during World War II it was not new to Canada.

24. D

The Canadian Charter of Rights and Freedoms is the supreme document that guaranatees all individual rights and freedoms in Canada. Freedom of Religion is one of the key aspects of the Charter has more importance than a provincial education act.

While all of the other acts listed are important, only the Charter of Rights and Freedoms governs all aspects ofcitizne's lives.

25. D

In the 1990s the French government began to restrict the display of religious symbols in public. This meant that public institutions, including schools, would not allow any display of religion.

26. B

Speaker II is most likely to oppose mercantilism and therefore share similar beliefs to Adam Smith. This person would believe in the free market system and laissez-faire economics.

27. B

Because of Speaker II's beliefs in the free market system, Adam Smith would most likely agree with him because of their shared economic beliefs.

28. A

John Stuart Mill would most likely have agreed with the statement made by Speaker I. His well know work *On Liberty* is a foundation of modern liberal thought. It states the belief that each individual is free to do as he or she chooses, as long as no harm is done to others.

29. C

The given headlines are all examples of illiberal ideas and actions carried out by the Canadian government during different time periods.

30. B

In 2008, Prime Minister Stephen Harper formally apologized for the abuses carried out by the residential school system and for the devastating effects this had on aboriginal children and their families.

31. D

The politician is advocating the end to a monopoly and giving the farmers a choice in how they market their crops. These actions and beliefs are similar to those represented in classical liberalism. The key factors being freedom of choice and as little government involvement as possible in people's lives.

The other choices focus on government involvement in the economy so that the whole nation is protected and not just one group. While neo-conservatism would be close, it is an ideology that does reject both classical and modern liberalism at times.

32. A

Farmer 1 is an advocate of classical liberalism because of the opportunity for choice. He therefore supports the government because it will give him that choice and not be restricted to selling his crop to only one company.

There is no indication that this action will provide for increased markets and guaranteed prices and less competition are already features of the current Wheat Board structure.

33. B

Farmer 2 believes that their rights are being taken away in this legislation. He thinks this because farmers are being ignored and that their elected voice is not being heard. This is all happening, in his view, through government actions that could be considered as illiberal.

While the government action could be considered as authoritarian it is not because it is a valid law being enacted by the Government of Canada.

34. A

Because the prime minister is shown as pulling the pin and letting the rail car, representing the Canadian Wheat Board, go off by itself it can be interpreted as an uncaring act. The idea represented here is that he does not care where it goes.

35. C

Since the rail car is represented as going careening down a hill and off the tracks it is symbolizing that it will go nowhere and most likely will not survive in the future.

The car is not plunging into the unknown because the actions by the government have indicated that they do not want the Canadian Wheat Board to survive.

36. B

Speaker II represents Joseph Stalin. His five-year plans, which resulted in the famine in Ukraine and his purging of those who opposed him, caused the deaths of millions of people.

37. B/C

Speaker I represents Lenin because he was the one wanted a violent revolution to overthrow the government at that time. As well he is the person associated with instituting the New Economic Policy. Speaker III represents Hitler because he created the National Socialist German Workers' Party and he believed in the natural superiority of the German people.

38. B

Speaker IV most likely represents a Ukrainian farmer who lived through the Ukrainian *Holodomor*. The famine and the resulting deaths in Ukraine were orchestrated by Stalin and his five-year plans. He used the fertile soil and crops of Ukraine to fund the Russian economy, and he used the famine and deaths of Ukrainians to quell the rising Ukrainian national sentiment.

39. A

The unnamed shaded countries are North America and a majority of the countries in Europe. These are the countries that make up the North Atlantic Treaty Organization or NATO.

NORAD involves only North America and the WHO and the WTO are worldwide organizations.

40. A

Over time a number of the countries that were not shaded formed to become the Non-Aligned Movement.

They did this because they did not want to side with the East or the West because they believed that neither one of the two existing groups really represented their needs and aspirations. This happened in 1955 and at its founding was composed of mainly African and Asian countries.

41. D

Speaker 1 implies that their actions are pushing one's demands to the point of threatening military action and forcing a showdown between two nations. This is the classic definition of brinkmanship.

42. A

The allusion in the quote here is that even though two countries may have differences and may not get along it is better to agree to disagree and recognize the differences rather than take an action, such as war, in order to force a point of view. This is the definition of detente.

43. C

A careful reading of all four sources indicates that they are all referring to the Soviet Union. With Source 1 referring to brinkmanship, Source 2 referring to detente and Source 3 pointing to totalitarian regimes it strongly is hinting at the Soviet Union. Source 4 rounds this out with the mention of the "iron curtain" which was the term that was used to describe the separation of the West from the Soviet Union and its satellites.

None of the other mentioned countries meets all of the references mentioned in the four sources.

44. A

The character carrying the missile in the cartoon is an example of deterrence. He mentions that the missile is a negotiating tool which hints at the fact that he will use it to force the people that he is negotiating to accept his ideas or not push their own for fear that he may use the missile.

While all of the other terms have some relevance to the cartoon and could go beyond the cartoon it is focussing on the act of deterrence.

45. A

All of the references and representations in the quotes and the cartoons all are referring to an era that was known as the Cold War. This is the over arching term used to describe this era.

While the Korean War and the Vietnam War happened during this time period they are only incidents that happened during the Cold War.

46. B

The shifting ideas about the economy which spurred the Industrial Revolution included the idea that commodities rather than gold and silver held the most value so finding efficient ways to produce these commodities become very important.

47. B

Edmund Burke is considered to be the father of conservatism under which traditions are valued and should be maintained while still recognizing the need for some change as society evolves.

Burke was not supportive of radical change, returning to the past or preventing new ideas and change.

48. D

Unlike many people of his era, Mill believed that if provided with the right opportunities, women could contribute as much as men and that society as a whole would be better for it.

Each of the other statements would likely be supported by Mill.

49. D

A free-market (capitalist) economy is characterized by each of the examples provided. Citizens are expected to provide for themselves, and the government has a very limited role in the workings of the economy.

Although in a mixed economy, there is somewhat of an expectation of self sufficiency, a social safety net exists for those in need of support and the government has more of a role in the economy. In a command economy, the government regulates industry and provides for its citizens through public ownership of the means of production and property. A traditional economy is one which generally existed before industrialization, usually based on agriculture where people work collectively to provide for the whole and labour is distributed according to traditional roles.

50. C

The Haudenosaunee Confederacy is believed to be one of the first groups to outline the given points as part of their political system.

51. D

Edmund Burke, a British member of Parliament in the mid- to late -18th century, is considered to be the father of modern conservatism. He lived at the height of the Enlightenment, but much preferred a political ideology based on strong principles, traditions and morality.

52. C

In Canada, the Canadian Charter of Rights and Freedoms overrules any other law or decision.

53. A

The ideas described are ones that are attributed to John Stuart Mill. He was interested in the protection of individual freedom and the promotion of individual decision making as the core to societal institutions. The ideas represented in the question represent his thinking from him book, "On Liberty".

54. B

The thoughts presented in the correct response are those attributed to Jean-Jacques Rousseau. His ideal state was one where the general will of the people was the absolute authority. He believed that citizens should make the laws directly. These thoughts were based on his belief that men were basically good and equal.

55. B

In the Canadian government system the Upper Chamber or the Senate is composed of individuals who have been appointed by the Prime Minister. This situation has always had its critics because as a result a portion of the people involved in making laws in Canada are not elected by the population at large and therefore this can be seen as undemocratic.

56. A

After the Cuban Missile Crisis almost brought the two major super powers at the time, the United States and the Soviet Union, to a war that could have resulted in the first nuclear war cooler heads prevailed. While the Cold War continued these two countries worked at not getting to that point again. They did this trough diplomacy, arms talks and reductions and cultural exchanges.

The other choices are all terms related to the Cold War. They are mainly words that are associated with the tensions at the time and not necessarily related to the reduction of tensions.

57. D

President Harry Truman was the first President of the United States to deal with the Cold War and the spread of Soviet communist influence around the world. He wanted to stop this spread, and instead of having a hot war Truman tried to create alliances and provide aid to countries who did not want to be part of the Soviet sphere.

58. B

In response to the Soviet Union becoming a nuclear power, Canada, the United States and most of the countries of Western Europe formed an alliance to deal with the potential threat of a nuclear attack from the Soviet Union.

Answer B refers to the DEW line that was established by NORAD at the same time as the creation of NATO but it was a separate organization that involved mainly Canada and the United States. Answer C is not true and D was carried out by the United States and the Soviet Union.

59. C

Ronald Reagan was President of the United States for most of the 1980's. As a Republican President one of his main goals was less government in the economy. He advocated less personal and business taxes with increased military spending. This theory is also known as supply-side economics or trickle-down economics.

60. D

The New Economic Policy is a Russian program that is associated with Vladimir Lenin. It was his attempt to help right the Soviet economy in its early years. This program was abandoned by Stalin when he came to power and was replaced by the Five-Year Plans.

Appendices

GLOSSARY OF TERMS

Aboriginal A person whose racial group has inhabited a particular geographic region since before recorded history.

antiballistic missile system A system designed to intercept and destroy incoming ballistic missiles before they can reach their targets.

bill of rights A list of the rights and freedoms considered essential in a nation. Bills of rights often form part of a nation's constitution.

boom-bust cycle Alternating periods of economic prosperity (boom) and depression (bust); also known as the economic or business cycle.

boycott A refusal to conduct business with a particular person, business, nation, or other such entity.

brinkmanship A military or political ploy in which a nation deliberately moves to the brink of open warfare in order to intimidate an opponent.

civil disobedience An act of protest in which a person or group deliberately breaks a law in order to highlight an injustice. Civil disobedience is nonviolent, and protesters are generally careful to avoid escalation.

civil liberty A liberty that protects citizens from unwarranted government interference. Civil liberties are the core liberal freedoms: freedom of speech, freedom of the press, etc.

collectivism A broad ideology in which individual rights and freedoms are secondary to the good of the community as a whole.

command economy An economy that is thoroughly controlled by the state.

common good The ideal of the greatest good for the greatest number of people.

communal property Any property held in common by a collective or commune.

communism A radical form of socialism in which the means of production are controlled by small collective units, or communes.

concentration camp A camp in which people of a common race, ethnicity, religion, or other such factor are grouped together. Since the Second World War, concentration camps are frequently associated with death camps, in which the purpose is to murder those gathered in the camp.

constitution A nation's foundational code of laws and principles of government.

culture The common patterns of behaviour and modes of expression of a society.

détente An easing of tensions; in the context of the Cold War, the period lasting from the beginning of the Nixon administration (1969) to the Soviet invasion of Afghanistan (1979).

environmentalism An ideology that opposes the harm or abuse of natural ecosystems.

franchise The legal ability to vote.

Governor General Canada's formal head of state and representative of the British monarch; the Governor General assents to the recommendations of Parliament or the prime minister, except in rare cases.

House of Commons In Canada, the lower house of Parliament. Its membership comprises elected members of Parliament and includes the prime minister and his or her cabinet.

humanitarian crisis A situation in which people are unable to obtain or maintain the basic necessities of life.

ideology A collection of ideas and beliefs, generally relating to politics, society, and economics.

individualism A broad ideology in which the rights and freedoms of individuals are of primary importance.

industrialism The period in which a society moves toward machine-assisted agriculture, manufacturing, and transportation; more or less synonymous with the term *Industrial Revolution*.

internment The imprisonment of a group of people who have not been convicted of a crime; these people are generally interned because they are deemed a threat.

invisible hand Adam Smith's term for the unintentional and beneficial consequences of self-interest.

kulaks In the Soviet Union, a class of rich peasants created under Lenin's New Economic Policy.

laissez-faire An economic stance that opposes any government interference in the economy.

liberal democracy A democracy in which citizens are guaranteed core civil liberties.

liberalism 1. An ideology that promotes individual rights and freedoms, largely based on the works of John Stuart Mill and Adam Smith. 2. A political stance that lies at or near the centre of the political spectrum.

MAD Mutual Assured Destruction; in the context of the Cold War, the understanding that one superpower could not attack the other without being destroyed by the retaliation.

means of production Any tool, machine, vehicle, or other item used to produce material goods.

media The way in which information is spread within a society.

member of Parliament An official elected to represent his or her constituents in the House of Commons of the Canadian Parliament.

mercantilism An economic stance, prevalent in the 16th through 18th centuries, that was characterized by frequent government interference in the economy and the accumulation of bullion (precious metals).

nationalism An ideology that promotes the importance of the nation; frequently manifested in displays of patriotism.

NATO The North Atlantic Treaty Organization; a mutual defence organization comprising the United States and its allies.

NKVD The Soviet secret police force during the reign of Josef Stalin.

pandemic An infectious disease that has spread throughout a nation or multiple nations.

Parliament of Canada The seat of the Canadian government. Parliament comprises two houses: the House of Commons and the Senate.

Pentagon, the The headquarters of the United States Department of Defence.

political spectrum A comparison of political ideologies that places conservative ideologies on the right and socialist ideologies on the left. Communism is at the extreme left; fascism is at the extreme right.

prime minister The leader of the political party with the most seats in the House of Commons; therefore, the head of government (but not head of state, which is technically the Governor General).

private property Property that belongs to an individual, business, charity, church, or other such organization. Private property is protected by law in liberal democracies, meaning that it cannot be legally taken, used, consumed, or trespassed upon without the owner's consent.

progressive taxation A system of taxation wherein the percentage of income taken as tax increases in proportion to income; in other words, the rich pay a higher percentage of tax than the poor.

proliferation To increase in number and spread. During the Cold War, the proliferation of nuclear weapons was a major concern.

proxy battle A battle in which, instead of clashing directly, warring powers support those who fight on their behalf (i.e., as proxies). For example, a battle between US-backed revolutionaries and a Soviet-backed government would be a proxy battle.

public property Property that can be used by any member of the public; public property is generally controlled and maintained by the state or a representative of the state.

purge Large-scale elimination of political opponents through various means, including execution, exile, and imprisonment.

religion A system of belief about the nature of the universe and humanity's place within it.

reparations Payments made to a nation to compensate it for the financial costs of a war.

residential school A school intended to assimilate Aboriginal children into European-based society.

rule of law The principle whereby the rulers of a nation are still subject to the laws of that nation.

Senate The upper house of the Canadian Parliament, comprising members appointed by the Governor General on the recommendation of the prime minister. The Senate rarely overturns legislation that has been approved in the House of Commons.

social pressure Attempts to get people to change their behaviour without resorting to more overt forms of coercion.

social tyranny The social pressure in a society to have everyone conform to the mainstream view.

socialism An ideology that calls for increased government control in the economy, collective control of the means of production, and economic equality among individuals.

sovereignty The independence of a nation or other political entity.

soviet A collective unit comprising workers, farmers, and soldiers; soviets were the basic political union of the Soviet Union.

sphere of influence An area under the direct or indirect domination of a superpower.

spirituality A personal view of the nature of the universe and humanity's place within it.

strategic arms Weapons intended to cause damage over a large area. Today, such weapons are commonly referred to as WMD (weapons of mass destruction).

superpower A nation that is extremely powerful in multiple areas, especially politics, economics, and military.

terrorism The use of violence, or the threat of violence, against civilians in order to create an atmosphere of terror. The goal of terrorism is generally to intimidate societies or governments into changing their policies.

totalitarianism A form of government in which the ruler or ruling body has absolute power over the nation.

trade union An organization comprising labourers who work in the same or similar occupations, generally formed to give those labourers more power in dealing with their employers or the government.

tyranny Oppressive and often arbitrary exercise of power, generally political.

tyranny of the majority A situation in which the majority acts without consideration for the views or needs of a minority.

USA PATRIOT Act USA PATRIOT is an acronym for **U**niting and **S**trengthening **A**merica by **P**roviding **A**ppropriate **T**ools **R**equired to **I**ntercept and **O**bstruct **T**errorism. The USA PATRIOT Act was passed in the wake of the terrorist attacks of September 11, 2001, and greatly expanded the powers of law enforcement in the United States.

Warsaw Pact 1. A mutual defence agreement signed by the Soviet Union and the Communist nations of Eastern Europe. 2. The bloc of nations that signed the agreement.

CREDITS

ORDERING INFORMATION

SCHOOL ORDERS

Schools and school jurisdictions are eligible for our educational discount rate. Contact Castle Rock Research for more information.

THE KEY **Study Guides** are specifically designed to assist students in preparing for unit tests, final exams, and provincial examinations.

THE KEY **Study Guides**—$29.95 each plus G.S.T.

SENIOR HIGH		JUNIOR HIGH	ELEMENTARY
Biology 30	Biology 20	English Language Arts 9	English Language Arts 6
Chemistry 30	Chemistry 20	Mathematics 9	Mathematics 6
English 30-1	English 20-1	Science 9	Science 6
English 30-2	Mathematics 20-1	Social Studies 9	Social Studies 6
Mathematics 30-1	Physics 20	Mathematics 8	Mathematics 4
Mathematics 30-2	Social Studies 20-1	Mathematics 7	English Language Arts 3
Physics 30	English 10-1		Mathematics 3
Social Studies 30-1	Mathematics 10		
Social Studies 30-2	Combined		
	Science 10		
	Social Studies 10-1		

Student Notes and Problems (SNAP) Workbooks contain complete explanations of curriculum concepts, examples, and exercise questions.

SNAP Workbooks—$29.95 each plus G.S.T.

SENIOR HIGH		JUNIOR HIGH	ELEMENTARY
Biology 30	Biology 20	Mathematics 9	Mathematics 6
Chemistry 30	Chemistry 20	Science 9	Mathematics 5
Mathematics 30-1	Mathematics 20-1	Mathematics 8	Mathematics 4
Mathematics 30-2	Physics 20	Science 8	Mathematics 3
Mathematics 31	Mathematics 10	Mathematics 7	
Physics 30	Combined	Science 7	
	Science 10		

Class Notes and Problem Solved—$19.95 each plus G.S.T.

SENIOR HIGH		JUNIOR HIGH
Biology 30	Biology 20	Mathematics 9
Chemistry 30	Chemistry 20	Science 9
Mathematics 30-1	Mathematics 20-1	Mathematics 8
Mathematics 30-2	Physics 20	Science 8
Mathematics 31	Mathematics 10 Combined	Mathematics 7
Physics 30		Science 7

Visit our website for a tour of resource content and features or order resources online at
www.castlerockresearch.com/store/

#2410, 10180 – 101 Street NW
Edmonton, AB Canada T5J 3S4
e-mail: learn@castlerockresearch.com

Phone: 780.448.9619
Toll-free: 1.800.840.6224
Fax: 780.426.3917

ORDER FORM

THE KEY

THE KEY	QUANTITY
Biology 30	
Chemistry 30	
English 30-1	
English 30-2	
Mathematics 30-1	
Mathematics 30-2	
Physics 30	
Social Studies 30-1	
Social Studies 30-2	
Biology 20	
Chemistry 20	
English 20-1	
Mathematics 20-1	
Physics 20	
Social Studies 20-1	
English 10-1	
Math 10 Combined	
Science 10	
Social Studies 10-1	
Social Studies 9	
English Language Arts 9	
Mathematics 9	
Science 9	
Mathematics 8	
Mathematics 7	
English Language Arts 6	
Mathematics 6	
Science 6	
Social Studies 6	
Mathematics 4	
Mathematics 3	
English Language Arts 3	

Student Notes and Problems Workbooks

Student Notes and Problems Workbooks	QUANTITY SNAP Workbooks
Mathematics 31	
Biology 30	
Chemistry 30	
Mathematics 30-1	
Mathematics 30-2	
Physics 30	
Biology 20	
Chemistry 20	
Mathematics 20-1	
Physics 20	
Mathematics 10 Combined	
Science 10	
Mathematics 9	
Science 9	
Mathematics 8	
Science 8	
Mathematics 7	
Science 7	
Mathematics 6	
Mathematics 5	
Mathematics 4	
Mathematics 3	

Problem Solved and Class Notes

Problem Solved and Class Notes	QUANTITY Class Notes	QUANTITY Problem Solved
Mathematics 31		
Biology 30		
Chemistry 30		
Mathematics 30-1		
Mathematics 30-2		
Physics 30		
Biology 20		
Chemistry 20		
Mathematics 20-1		
Physics 20		
Mathematics 10 Combined		
Mathematics 9		
Science 9		
Mathematics 8		
Science 8		
Mathematics 7		
Science 7		

Total Cost

Subtotal 1	
Subtotal 2	
Subtotal 3	
Cost Subtotal	
Shipping and Handling*	
G.S.T	
Order Total	

*(Please call for current rates)

PAYMENT AND SHIPPING INFORMATION

Name: _____
School _____
Telephone: _____

SHIP TO
School Code: _____
School: _____
Address: _____
City: _____ Postal Code: _____

PAYMENT
☐ By credit card   VISA/MC
Number: _____
Expiry Date: _____
Name on card: _____
☐ Enclosed cheque
☐ Invoice school   P.O. number: _____

CASTLE ROCK
RESEARCH CORP

#2410, 10180 – 101 Street NW, Edmonton, AB T5J 3S4   **Phone:** 780.448.9619 **Fax:** 780.426.3917
Email: learn@castlerockresearch.com   **Toll-free:** 1.800.840.6224
www.castlerockresearch.com